The Awakening That Must Come

Lewis A. Drummond

BROADMAN PRESS
Nashville, Tennessee

4265–35
ISBN: 0–8054–6535–9

Dewey Decimal Classification: 269
Subject heading: EVANGELISTIC WORK

Library of Congress Catalog Card Number: 78–059239
Printed in the United States of America.

Dedicated to

My dear Mother and late Father
who gave of themselves under God
so that I had an early homelife
that has been a rich source of
blessing wherever God has led me.

Contents

*I rose from my fasting . . . and fell upon
my knees and spread out my hands to the Lord
my God, saying:*

*O my God, I am ashamed and blush to lift
up my face to thee, my God, for our iniquities
have risen higher than our heads, and our
guilt has mounted to the heavens.*

*But now for a brief moment favor has been
shown by the Lord our God, to leave us a
remnant. . . .*

*Our God has not forsaken us in our bondage,
but has extended to us his steadfast love . . .
to grant us some reviving to set up the house
of our God.*

[EZRA 9:5–6, 8, RSV]

Foreword

Fresh winds of the Spirit are blowing through the church. There is a sense of expectancy in the air. Multitudes of people, tired of merely going through the forms of respectable religion, are yearning for something that will put vibrancy in their souls, and many are coming alive to the claims of Christ.

Certainly we can be grateful for the positive movements of spiritual quest in our midst, but a deeper and more pervasive work of God still awaits us—an infusion of holy love that will engulf the whole body of believers and will reach into the total fabric of our life and culture.

This book helps us appreciate the challenge. Through an in-depth look at major contemporary renewal movements, their strengths and weaknesses, it points beyond these beginnings to a more profound revival to come.

Bringing realism to the study, the author analyzes some notable awakenings of the past, focusing on spiritual principles that shaped their course and result. Particular attention is given to the Puritan-Pietist movements that brought experiential faith and evangelistic fervor into the Reformation of Europe, moving across the ocean to have a mighty impact on the church in America.

The form great awakenings take, of course, varies with each generation. God always tailors his work to the situation. But by learning how revivals have come in other periods of history, we can better understand what is happening today

In these pages, Dr. Lewis Drummond, the Billy Graham Professor of Evangelism at Southern Baptist Seminary, shares his distilled insights from years of study and teaching on the subject. Though this work is not exhaustive, he probes deep with a scholar's objectivity. And, with all his erudition, he has not lost the concern of a shepherd nor the urgency of an evangelist. That is why, in the end, this is not a treatise to inform but a summons to act.

I recall the German pastor Pregizer of Haiterboch, once seeking to arouse his lethargic congregation by suddenly shouting in an Easter Monday sermon: "Fire! Fire! Fire!"

"Where?" the startled congregation asked.

Whereupon the pastor exclaimed, "In disciples' hearts."

To be sure, that is where we must all face the issue. Revival comes in the hearts of God's people. And it is there where each one of us finally must become combustible material for the flame of God to consume.

May the message of this book be used of the Spirit to ignite our faith and move us to our knees.

ROBERT E. COLEMAN
Professor of Evangelism

Asbury Theological Seminary
Wilmore, Kentucky

Introduction

Immorality is rocketing at an alarming rate; divorce, drugs, crime in the streets, white-collar defrauding, pornography, indiscriminate abortions, and a million other attempts to flaunt the laws of God shock us into an awareness of the seriousness of the hour. So scream the seers and so prophesy the prophets—and not without statistics to prove their point! The entire western world is being engulfed by a tidal wave of secularism if not outright godlessness.

And there stands the church—the bulwark. Yet the critics cry that the church itself is going down for the count. Whatever happened to the strength and moral fiber the Christian community formally injected into the stream of society? Where is the standard it used to raise? Where is the voice that used to be heard? Is the contemporary church really inept and incapable of doing anything about our headlong plunge into a moral abyss that will inevitably spell destruction? Are the people of God still able to be the "salt of the earth" who can evangelize our generation, preserve a viable society, and bring great glory to God, or are we doomed? It surely seems that the church is fast loosing ground and influence in the power structures of today's turbulent society, not to mention the church's prime task—world evangelization.

Yet, paradoxically, there are other prophets who tell us a great spiritual awakening is dawning in America. These prophets are not found exclusively in the pulpits. George Gallup, the famous pollster, is so convinced a major religious

9

revival is already underway that he has set up a new office to investigate the phenomenon. He is calling it the Princeton Religion Research Center. The polls have actually revealed some startling facts.

- One American in three says he has been "born again."
- Half the Protestants and one-quarter of the Catholics have had a "mystical religious experience."
- People in high places openly testify to their faith—even the president of the United States.
- Fifty-six percent of the American people say religion is very important to them.
- Ninety-four percent of Americans believe in God.
- Perhaps most important of all, eighty percent of Americans would like to see a religious revival.

As one writer in *Psychology Today* put it, "America was born a God-obsessed nation, and continues to be one—a datum that certain professors find embarrassing" (April 1978, p. 74).

The reports are not confined to the American scene; secular Europe seems to be coming alive to a new thrust of the Spirit. Daniel Bell recently gave a lecture at the London School of Economics, University of London, on the theme of a new spiritual awakening. He said the next years may well produce a "return to the sacred." He contended a religious revival could soon break in, especially an awakening of what he termed "evangelical piety." Speaking like this in the crass secularism of the University of London School of Economics is most significant.

A series of radio programs was aired in Sweden and the general conviction was that secularism had reached its peak. Further, Dr. Visser t'Hooft of Sweden said, "We are now in a situation in which for many Europeans, especially the younger ones, a meeting with the gospel comes as a new discovery."

But how do we square all of this with the rocketing

rise of ungodly living? Perhaps this is the answer: Through this new interest in religion, God is preparing the ground, breaking up the soil, sowing the seed to give America, and hopefully the whole western world, a great, new, spiritual revival. Just waiting to burst on the scene with the shock and impact of a sudden, summer thunderstorm, there may be a great awakening. Surely we all wish this could be true. Unless something like this does break in on the scene, despite the current popularity of Christianity, I see little hope for a continuing, workable society and a dynamic, evangelizing church. We need desperately a mighty move of God upon us.

A great new revival, transcending even the Great Awakening of 1734, is the theme of this book. I shall attempt to define, analyze, relate history, and lay out the principles of spiritual revivals and how they occur. I trust I shall not be presumptuous, but I also want to make suggestions as to what God's people can do to be his instruments in a new awakening for the glory of Jesus Christ.

It is my earnest prayer that this small volume may in some way be used by God to make its contribution toward the dawning of a new spiritual revival. If such be the case, my efforts will be amply rewarded.

I must express my appreciation to those whose help was invaluable in the preparation of this work. Mrs. Kay Furse labored over her typewriter preparing the original draft. The girls in Office Services at Southern Seminary prepared the final copy. My wife Betty, faithfully as always, did the final proofreading. Many others made helpful suggestions. To all these I express my sincere gratitude.

This book goes forth, placed in the hand of the One who gives spiritual revival, with the prayer he will use it to bring honor to his name in the dawning of a great awakening.

1
It Happened Once; Can It Happen Again?

We would hardly have called him a dynamic preacher. He laboriously read every word from a manuscript. Not only that, his eyesight and writing were so poor he held the manuscript only inches from his nose, rarely looking at the congregation. The message was Calvinistic and hell fire! Not much to inspire excitement, yet his hearers writhed in an agony of conviction to the point of crying aloud for mercy as more than one completely passed out. The preacher droned on, still they came by the multitudes. What is the answer to this unbelievable drama?

The preacher was Jonathan Edwards. The time and place was 1734 in Northampton, Massachusetts. The event was the initial Great American Awakening. The answer is God was reviving his people.

The First Great Awakening

No event in early American life is of more spiritual significance than what we now call the First Great Awakening. It reversed the course of history, sacred and secular. The colonies were never quite the same again. Jonathan Edwards, the personification of the revival, was a remarkable character. Intellectually he had few peers; philosophers consider him the first scintillating thinker in American thought. An ardent student, he had a brilliant mind, ending his career as president of Princeton University.

Although Edwards' preaching proceeded out of his thoroughgoing Calvinism, he preached with great persuasion to win people to Christ. Hear him thunder out in his most famous sermon, "Sinners in the Hands of an Angry God":

> O sinner! consider the fearful danger you are in. 'Tis a great furnace of wrath, a wide and bottomless pit, full of the fire of wrath, that you are held over in the hand of that God whose wrath is provoked and incensed as much against many of the damned in hell. You hang by a slender thread, with the flames of divine wrath flashing about it, and ready every moment to singe it and burn it asunder; and you have no interest in any Mediator, and nothing to lay hold of to save yourself, nothing to keep off the flames of wrath, nothing of your own, nothing that you ever have done, nothing that you can do, to induce God to spare you one moment.
>
> Therefore let every one that is out of Christ now awake and fly from the wrath to come. The wrath of Almighty God is now undoubtedly hanging over a great part of this congregation. Let every one fly out of Sodom. "Haste and escape for your lives, look not behind you, escape to the mountain, lest ye be consumed." [1]

Mightily moved by the power of the Holy Spirit, it is understandable why people were so deeply convicted by Edwards' preaching, even if his style left much to be desired.

Edwards was not the only revival preacher in the Great Awakening. Many pulpits shook under the preaching of men like Gilbert Tennent, James Davenport, John Rowland, Shubal Stearns, and no less a personage than George Whitefield, British Puritan of power. Whitefield sailed the Atlantic to the New World many times, profoundly influencing people as diverse as the staunch Puritans and Benjamin Franklin. He died on his eleventh preaching tour of America and is buried under the pulpit of the Presbyterian Church in Newburyport, Massachusetts.

Through these great personalities and scores of others, thousands were converted. The church returned to apostolic simplicity. The whole moral and political atmosphere of the colonies was radically purified. Even secular historians eulogize those days. It was God's great hour for early America.

But the movement subsided like the ebb and flow of

the ocean tide. The Revolution came and passed; life was rugged. Then quite suddenly God again showered down his Spirit. This time God visited the South, and the Second Great Awakening erupted with the force of an exploding volcano.

The Second Great Awakening

In the late 1780s another great surge of revival power swept the newly formed United States. As the First Awakening had its beginnings among New England Congregationalists and Presbyterians, the Second Awakening broke out in Methodist and Baptist circles in Virginia and soon spread to the Carolinas. Although it began as a Baptist and Methodist movement, the Presbyterians and others were not exempt. Caught up in the awakening were two North Carolina Presbyterian ministers, James McGready and his protégé Barton Stone.

McGready and Stone were destined to be greatly used by God. Trekking through the Cumberland Gap, they took up their ministries in Kentucky. James McGready, after two or three years in Tennessee, settled in Logan County, Kentucky, and began preaching at the Red River Meeting House in 1800.

McGready was an "impassioned preacher, diligent pastor, and fervent man of prayer." [2] In June of 1800 he called on the people of South-Central Kentucky to gather for an extended four-day observance of the Lord's Supper. People came in expectation of blessings, and God met their faith. The Holy Spirit fell on them powerfully. Friday and Saturday saw floods of repentant tears and then times of exuberant rejoicing. The Spirit moved even deeper on Sunday when the Lord's Supper was served. The climax came on the final day when John McGee, a Methodist minister, gave the closing exhortation. His own words describe the scene.

I . . . exhorted them to let the Lord omnipotent reign in their hearts, and submit to him, and their souls should live . . . I turned again and losing sight of fear of man, I went through the house shouting and exhorting with all possible ecstasy and energy, and the floor was soon covered by the slain.[3]

People had come in unprecedented numbers from a hundred-mile radius of Red River. Because the multitudes could not be housed in the existing building in the community, they brought bed rolls and tents in their wagons, and the first camp meeting occurred. It was all quite unplanned, but a new movement and methodology was born.

What an experience it must have been to witness those days! McGready tells us:

No person seemed to wish to go home—hunger and sleep seemed to affect nobody—eternal things were the vast concern. Here awakening and converting work was to be found in every part of the multitude. . . . Sober professors, who had been communicants for many years, now lying prostrate on the ground, crying out in such language as this: 'O! how I would have despised any person a few days ago, who would have acted as I am doing now! But I cannot help it!' . . . persons of every description, white and black, were to be found in every part of the multitude . . . crying out for mercy in the most extreme distress.[4]

The Cane Ridge Revival

Of the people there, none was singled out by God for more usefulness than Barton Stone. He had been preaching at the Cane Ridge Meeting House in Bourbon County, Kentucky, invited and urged to serve there by Daniel Boone. Stone was so overwhelmed with the Red River revival that he went home and in May of 1801 called for a similar meeting at Cane Ridge. The work began and many were blessed. He called for another meeting in August, and to the utter astonishment of all, over 20,000 people arrived for the six-day camp meeting. It was an incredible event, for this was the sparsely populated frontier.

Among the thousands converted was James B. Finley, who later became a Methodist circuit rider. He wrote:

The noise was like the roar of Niagara. The vast sea of human beings seemed to be agitated as if by a storm. I counted seven ministers, all preaching at one time, some on stumps, others in wagons, and one was standing on a tree which had, in falling, lodged against another. . . . Some of the people were singing, others praying, some crying for mercy in the most piteous accents, while others were shouting most vociferously. While witnessing these scenes, a peculiarly-strange sensation, such as I had never felt before, came over me. My heart beat tumultously, my knees trembled, my lips quivered, and I felt as though I must fall to the ground. A strange supernatural power seemed to pervade the entire mass of mind there collected. . . . I stepped up on to a log, where I could have a better view of the surging sea of humanity. The scene that then presented itself to my mind was indescribable. At one time I saw at least five hundred swept down in a moment, as if a battery of a thousand guns had been opened upon them and then immediately followed shrieks and shouts that rent the very heavens.[5]

The American frontier was set ablaze. The Presbyterians and Methodists immediately caught fire, and the flame soon broke out among the Baptists in Carroll County on the Ohio River. Great personalities emerged from the awakening, such as Peter Cartwright and the Methodist circuit riders. Baptist revivalism, which continues to this day, had its birth in this movement. The camp meeting motif of evangelism spread all over eastern America. The entire frontier was radically transformed. Instead of gambling, cursing, and vice, spirituality and genuine Christianity characterized the early westward movement. It was God's great hour

But like the First Great Awakening, the second also waned. The War of 1812 came and went and spiritual stagnation settled in.

The Great Nineteenth-Century Awakening

Then once more God came upon his people. One of the early outpourings came to a twenty-nine-year-old, brilliant, but skeptical, lawyer in western New York state. God gripped the unbelieving heart of the young barrister. Here is his own account.

I was powerfully converted on the morning of the 10th of October, 1821. In the evening of the same day I received overwhelming baptisms (infillings) of the Holy Ghost, that went through me, as it seemed to me, body and soul. I immediately found myself endowed with such power from on high that a few words dropped here and there to individuals were the means of their immediate conversion.

His name? Charles G. Finney: revivalist, pastor, educator, social reformer, abolitionist, giant. No American preacher has preached with more power than he. Whole cities were converted under his ministry. He is almost a legend to those who know the impact of his life and work.

The move of God spread throughout the whole Northeast until the great prayer revival of 1858 gathered it all together and launched the widespread evangelistic ministry of D. L. Moody. Europe had its counterpart movement too, but that is another story. What glorious days they were!

Today's Great Need

However, in all such movements, it seems that spiritual deadness inevitably creeps in like a grim reaper cutting down the blessed results of the revival. Except for a few isolated places, such as Wheaton College in Illinois and Asbury College in Kentucky, twentieth-century American Christianity has been strangely bereft of these deep movements of the Holy Spirit. Although a significant interest in church life developed in the late forties and fifties, the social unrest and Vietnam affair in the sixties soon scuttled that movement.

Few of us today have ever seen a widespread spiritual awakening. Blessings here and there, yes; but, oh, for an awakening that would bring the masses to the cross and revolutionize our churches and nation. This is the cry of many. Its echoes are the cry of my heart.

Is there any hope? Are there any harbingers of an awakening on the horizon? Can we expect to see it happen again? I am convinced the Holy Spirit is at work to that end. I am sure he is trying to break through once again. We could perhaps be on the verge of the Third Great Awakening. Why do I feel that way? First, because God has always periodically revived his work. Secondly, I am encouraged because of what is taking place in three significant contemporary movements that just may be the beginnings of the kind of awakening we need. We turn our attention to an investigation of these important movements in an attempt to answer the basic question, *Can it happen again?*

2
Renewed, Revitalized, Rededicated

"The Lord has started a great work among some Methodist laymen in Florida," a preacher told me. That was one of my first introductions to the modern renewal movement. It grabbed my imagination. I was the pastor of a church that sorely needed reviving. Moreover, I had been a student of spiritual awakenings since my seminary days. I became "all ears" as the preacher began to relate some of the things that were going on in this unusual Methodist congregation. It seemed lay people were coming alive as never before. Was a new, deep, profound revival rolling in like a tide? This was and is my pressing question. But before trying to answer this basic and essential query, we need to plow the historical ground that gave germination to this new spiritual harvest commonly called, *the Renewal Movement*.

The Roots of the Renewal Movement

It is almost impossible to search out all the sources of the modern renewal emphasis. I suppose the church has always in some sense attempted to renew itself. Yet a few streams can be explored that have fed into the surging river of enthusiasm.

Fifty years ago New York City began to hear a new voice. In the Calvary Episcopal Church, Sam Shoemaker preached so dynamically that people began to respond in unusual numbers. Unbelievers were converted and believers were spiritually deepened. It was then that Shoemaker hit on a fresh methodology to conserve the remarkable results.

Those making commitments were brought together to share with one another their new experiences and feelings. An informal testimony meeting was started. Every Thursday evening they met in the church's fellowship hall where they simply shared their spiritual discoveries.

All sorts of people with unbelievably different backgrounds came. The ministry was reaching across every cultural line. Shoemaker was convinced of the need of the kind of openness they were enjoying. Yet as the group grew, vast cultural differences began to hinder open sharing. So he grabbed on the idea of grouping people into compatible circles. In this setting they felt more secure in sharing their spiritual sojourn. Thus one of the first small-group movements in American Christianity was born, although Wesley had used this methodology earlier in England.

Great things germinated and grew in this fertile soil. For example, Bill Wilson was converted in a mission of the Calvary Church. Shoemaker got hold of him and placed him in a small supportive group. Wilson's concern was the alcoholic. Now that his own drinking problem was being solved, he was gripped with compassion for others. In this context, Wilson and Shoemaker put together the twelve steps that give victory to problem drinkers. Alcoholics Anonymous was born.

This small group movement met with monumental success, and it soon developed into what is now known as "Faith at Work." Something of this approach has been at the very core of the renewal movement ever since.

The Yokefellows

A second stream that fed into the widening renewal river is personified in Elton Trueblood. A dynamic Quaker and professor of philosophy at Earlham College in Indiana, Trueblood stands as almost the father figure of modern renewal thought.

A widespread movement began under Trueblood's impact. Known as The Yokefellows, conferences sprang up everywhere. The Yokefellows Conference Center in Richmond, Indiana, has become something of the Mecca of the contemporary emphasis.

Trueblood is an unusually gifted man and a voluminous author. He has written successfully in philosophy, ethics, family life, Bible studies, higher education, national affairs, and world peace. Yet he will always be remembered for his definitive works on church renewal. *Church* renewal; that is the key that unlocks his contribution. He has clearly seen that the *whole church,* not just individuals here and there, needs to be renewed. He tells us:

We cannot be Christians without the Church, for merely individual Christianity is a contradiction in terms. But, in spite of its greatness, the Church requires, at many points in its history, genuine renewal. . . . (It) goes stale unless there are small redemptive societies which grow up within it to arouse, to stimulate, and to revive.[1]

Individuals are renewed, of course. But the renewed must make their contribution to the entire church if renewal is to be meaningful. This is obviously a significant step forward from Shoemaker's more individualistic approach.

The Church of the Savior

A third stream that widens our renewal river flows out of the Church of the Savior in Washington, D. C. The pastor, Gordon Cosby, served as a military chaplain during World War II. After discharge from the service, he was disillusioned with the shallow spirituality of so many congregations. He decided to start all over again and build a church on the New Testament principles of discipline, dedication, and discipleship. He determined there would be, under God, at least one church that truly stood for something for the Savior.

The Church of the Savior has never become very large numerically. It is not hard to guess why. Few are willing to submit to the covenant demands for membership. Yet the impact of this congregation is tremendous. It has become

a parable church for many. It must unquestionably be
granted that the members of that church are deeply dedicated believers to the last person.

Moreover, mission has been mandatory in Cosby's philosophy. A church does not exist merely for mutual support
and spiritual growth; it must engage in ministry. It dare
not turn in on itself. Not that this emphasis has been entirely
absent in other renewal groups, but it is central in the
Church of the Savior. Elizabeth O'Conner's *Eighth Day of
Creation,* which tells of this church on mission, is an inspiration and challenge to any congregation. It is right here that
Cosby may have made his most lasting contribution to renewal emphasis.

Laity Lodge and Its Contribution

There is a fourth feeding stream to explore, Laity Lodge
in Texas. This retreat center started by a layman has forged
its contribution to renewal thought. Director Keith Miller,
while an able conference leader, will be best remembered
for his highly popular writings. His *Taste of New Wine* and
The Second Touch have been read over the world. Through
these books Miller has probably touched more average laymen than any other renewal personality. He has a beautiful
common touch that communicates to the concerned Christian. History may well view him as the most significant popularizer of the movement.

It must also be acknowledged that most major denominations, as well as individual personalities and churches, have
projected a significant input into our spiritual stream. Southern Baptists have directors of lay renewal in both the Evangelism Section of their Home Mission Board and in the Broth-
erhood Commission. The United Methodists have an
extensive Department of Discipleship, not to mention the
activity of the Presbyterians, Luthcrans, and many others.
Keen interest is also found among many Roman Catholics.
This movement is not stemming from isolated, religious reb-

els disillusioned with the establishment. It is influencing hundreds of thousands everywhere. The little early stream has become a surging river with rapids of enthusiasm and excitement for any brave oarsman wishing to challenge the waters.

Why has renewal found such a receptive riverbed in which to flow? Although the church always needs renewal, the great American ferment of the sixties no doubt forcefully pressed home an awareness of the anemia of many traditional structures and the shallow spirituality in too much of contemporary church life. The enthusiastic evangelism of the fifties began to dry up like a desert riverbed after a torrential downpour. Many became disillusioned, if not disgusted, with the church's seeming failure to respond to the tremendously pressing social perplexities of the day. America had become an urban, technical, sophisticated society. Yet most congregations continued to structure their programs on a rural basis, and the church almost seemed to be going down for the count. In this confusing mix, plus a thousand other deeply disturbing crosscurrents, those who loved the church began to cry out desperately for renewal. How was this heart cry met by the renewal movement?

Renewal's Answer

Five emphases can be gleaned from the renewal harvest. First, and foremost, it plows deep into the developing of discipleship. All the way from Shoemaker's early support groups to the current interest in Bonhoeffer's *Cost of Discipleship,* the movement has been conscientiously concerned with dynamic disciple making. All renewal groups strongly stress this need, some almost to a fault. If, for example, the Church of the Savior has made any mistakes, it is found in elevating church membership standards so high that some immature believers have been scared off. Still, we applaud, in principle, any appeal to make Jesus the Lord of all of life. The lordship of Christ is always the essence of a deep, maturing, spiritual experience.

Moreover, renewal's call to discipleship has reached all levels of people. Several years ago my path crossed that of a flight instructor at our local airport. He taught me to fly, so I got to know him quite well. He was a fine Christian man at the time but not particularly outgoing spiritually. I recently saw him again while holding an evangelistic campaign in his church. How he surprised me! He was aglow in the Spirit. My old flight instructor had obviously come alive to all that God has for a believer. He impressed me like the psalmist David who said, "As a hart longs for flowing streams, so longs my soul for thee, O God" (Ps. 42:1, RSV).

Would that all of God's people had such a thirst! For my friend, it all started through a renewal emphasis in his church. His whole spiritual life and outlook had been transformed. I find arguing with that very difficult.

Personal Relationships

Secondly, the development of deep, interpersonal, supportive relationships has been a central renewal theme. The biblical word *koinonia*, "fellowship," is at the core of the movement. Kittel says of this significant term:

Fellowship with Christ necessarily leads to fellowship with Christians, to the mutual fellowship of members of the community. . . . Paul uses . . . the idea of 'having a share' (that) often pass(es) over into that of 'giving a share.' This union and communion of Christians is quickened and expressed specifically under the pressure of sufferings; shared feeling moves over into the sharing of active assistance, it is the living bond in which the Christian stands.[2]

The renewed seem to have grasped the heart of this beautiful spiritual concept of sharing and mutual support. How different our churches would be if the members were warm and affirmative of each other—a real *koinonia*. What an impact they would make on society. I think we all agree with Trueblood when he said:

Once a church was a brave and revolutionary fellowship, changing the course of history by the introduction of discordant ideas; today it is a place where people go and sit on comfortable benches, waiting patiently until time to go home to their Sunday dinners.[3]

The Ministering Body

We all long to see our churches become that revolutionary fellowship. When a church does come alive, that is, becomes a true fellowship, there has always emerged the "abolition of the laity." This is the third emphasis of the renewal movement. Based on the "priesthood of all believers," the idea revolves around a fresh interpretation of Ephesians 4:11–12: "He gave some, apostles; and some, prophets; and some, evangelists; and some, pastors and teachers; For the perfecting of the saints, for the work of the ministry, for the edifying of the body of Christ." These verses have been traditionally understood as describing the role of professional ministers. The clergyman is to do the work of perfecting the saints, do the work of the ministry, and edify the body of Christ. But if we remove the second comma in verse 12, the whole picture changes. It now reads, the minister's role is to "perfect the saints unto the work of the ministry." In other words, the clergyman equips the saints to do the work. The real ministers in a church are the church members themselves—all of them. It is fully legitimate to remove this troublesome comma because there is no such punctuation in the early Greek text, and the prepositions demand its removal. Therefore, the real ministers in a local body of Christ are the entire body of saints. The professional, paid ministers are merely the equippers of the saints for their ministries. As Trueblood put it, the pastors, staff members, and so on are like the coaches of a ball team. The entire church "plays the game."

This basic approach of renewal has been discussed almost to death. Yet the principle is biblical, sensible, and important. It liberates the pastors for their real work, and it liberates the laity to discover and exercise their spiritual gift of ministry. In a word, it gets the whole church involved in service as a ministering body of Christ.

This principle has moved many churches to become the revolutionary fellowship Trueblood calls for. A classic case is the Peninsula Bible Church in Palo Alto, California. Pastor Ray Stedman has been building "Body Life"[4] for over thirty years in that great congregation. I heard him lecture on this central concept and how it operates among his people. It was thrilling. Here is a church that pulsates with vitality and effective service. We can hardly gainsay that.

Missions and Evangelism

"The evangelization of the world in our generation" is the church's goal, wrote A. T. Pierson many years ago. This "missionary watchword," as Pierson's challenge became known, has been a continuing source of inspiration to Christians. World evangelization is always our responsibility. *Everyone* has the right to hear the gospel intelligently presented at least once in their lives. Love demands that of the church; the Great Commission commands it. Yet it is here that the renewal movement's fourth contribution has been a mixed bag. There are renewal groups—and individuals—that are profoundly committed to share their faith. Others seem to need a spiritual shot in the arm to get them going in world evangelization. I know of a church that through its pastor has become deeply involved in renewal thought, yet it reaches very few for Christ. The members are hardly effective in even reaching their own children. They talk so much about an "evangelism of integrity" that they apparently forget to do any kind—good or bad. Others are in sharp contrast. In my own denomination, for example, the leadership of our lay-renewal work is grounded in our evangelism department. I warm to that approach.

Social Action

Lastly, renewal believes in penetrating society and being the salt of the earth to heal the hurts of a wounded world. This is to its credit. Trueblood tells us, "The church is at the very gates of hell itself, and even these will not be able to resist it." [5] The "gates" that will not prevail are "the gates of prejudices and hatred and ignorance and self-centeredness." [6] These bastions of evil must fall.

Most have come to see that a dualism between individual conversion and social action should have been buried long ago. The people of God do not have the luxury of making a convenient choice between these two areas of service. The Bible knows no such choice—nor should we. Great, growing churches in a quite natural way simply "find hurts and heal them," as Schuller put it.[7] People hurt spiritually, emotionally, physically, socially, and in a myriad of other ways. The true people of God step in and meet all these kinds of need. Here the renewal movement has tried to help us. I like that also.

The Centrality of Commitment

What is the sum of it all? I suppose it can be best put together in renewal's favorite word—*commitment.* Renewed people want a healthy church, and a church becomes robust in direct proportion to its commitment to Jesus Christ. He is Lord; therefore, he must become the Lord of life. And *lordship* is not a mere high-sounding, pious phrase in the renewal movement; they really mean it. Commitment and lordship combine into one broad, in-depth concept in renewal theology.

First, commitment means rejecting noninvolvement. Cool detachment that plays everything safe is sharply rejected. One must get involved in life, in the hurts of people, in the church—in the Lord himself. This means coming to know God personally. Being orthodox and religious is not enough. Walking with Jesus Christ *every day* is central. Further, this implies a life of self-discipline. Going to church on Sunday merely because it makes one "feel good" and doing nothing else until next Sunday will not suffice for the renewal movement. Christian commitment means disciplined Bible study, prayer, witnessing, righteous living, service to others, and all the other things Jesus stressed to his people in the Sermon on the Mount. In the light of the existential, undisciplined, emotional binge in which modern man indulges, I really respond to this reasoning.

Some Conclusions

It has now become quite clear that I feel very positive toward much in the contemporary renewal movement. However, there is also that which disturbs me.

To begin with, the lack of evangelistic and missionary zeal lurking in the wings of some renewal groups disappoints me. Their commitment to personal growth and social involvement is at times thrilling. But people without Jesus Christ as Lord and Savior flounder in desperate need—a need that makes all other needs pale in importance. Must we be reminded that sin cries for forgiveness; a new relationship with God needs to be established; the Holy Spirit's sealing and sanctifying work is vital; and eternal life is the highest goal? These are the issues that matter most. These are the needs that dominated the mind-set of the New Testament church. To downplay these facts is to miss the core of Christianity. Of course, all renewal groups do not give evangelism the subtle put-down I detect here and there, but enough do—or at least ignore the enterprise. This is a serious error. I would love to see a fresh vision of a worldwide witness dawn on the movement.

This leads to another problem, which may well be the real issue. The renewal movement has had some tendency to turn in on itself. It is easy to get so concerned about one's spiritual well-being that we forget the needy world out there. Thus an incipient kind of selfishness emerges that brings about an unhealthy concern for one's own spiritual life. This subtle move is especially true of the group aspect of the thrust. There is such comfort, support, and affirmation in a small group of like-minded people that one's whole world can easily begin to revolve around the self and those in the group. It can even degenerate into morbid introspective "navel gazing." And that can soon merge into a superior air that tends to look down on others who do not have the "courage" to be "real people" and share all experiences with their peer group regardless of how intimate those experiences may be. I was in a pastor's group on one occasion when one of the men began to try and lead us into something like that. I'm sure he meant well, but it backfired badly and brought nothing but dissension and hurt feelings. It did everything but heal. I hope this does not sound unduly judgmental; I know many in the movement who never degenerate into that kind of spiritual syndrome. Yet we must admit some do. When this happens, the individual, the church, let alone the world, is rarely served.

Another problem I see is the lack of biblical orientation in some renewal approaches. Although many renewal groups center themselves around the Scriptures, in some places and in very subtle ways the Bible takes a secondary seat. Personal experience becomes everything. I have read some renewal authors, and after a few chapters I longed for an appeal to the Word of God. The books came over more like psychological biographies rather than true biblical expressions of deep experiences of Jesus Christ. Our existential experiences are important, but they must grow out of and be judged by the objective Scriptures. If we do not tenaciously hold to that principle, sooner or later we get led up some mystical or psychological blind alley that can leave us disillusioned, if not defeated.

The Big Issue

There are many such issues. But there is one problem in the renewal movement that disturbs me most seriously. Yet, let it first be made clear again that I am warm to much in the thrust. It is obvious that many have genuinely matured in their faith and have become effective servants of Christ through renewal's emphasis. I thank God for each one! *But that is the quandary;* it has been just one here, one there, and a few over yonder that have been moved and deepened. At the most, we can search out only a small handful in most churches that are really alive and turned on to God through the renewal movement. What has happened to the overwhelming majority of God's people? Why hasn't the mainstream of the church been moved? After years of renewal promotion, most church members, as Sir John Lawrence said, still want "a building that looks like a church, services of the kind they're accustomed to, a clergyman dressed in the way they approve, *and to be left alone.*" Somehow, renewal has simply missed the bulk of God's people. And that is the prime problem!

The Real Answer?

How different the great historic spiritual awakenings have been. As already shown, the nineteenth-century frontier revival in Kentucky revolutionized the whole church—even all of society. The same happened in the Finney awakening. Hear his account of just one of the meetings that transformed Rome, New York.

The feeling was overwhelming. Some men of the strongest nerves were so cut down by the remarks which were made, that they were unable to help themselves, and had to be taken home by their friends. This meeting lasted till nearly night. It resulted in a great number of hopeful conversions, and was the means of greatly extending the work on every side. . . . The Spirit's work was so spontaneous, so powerful, and so overwhelming . . . no open immorality could be tolerated there for a moment . . . the town was full of prayer.[8]

The same phenomena occurred in the great Welsh Revival of 1902, the Hebrides awakening of 1949, ad infinitum. Awakenings transform everything they touch.

That is the kind of movement we need. That, I am sure, is what God wants to give. Oh, that it would happen in our day. It can, you know. I am absolutely convinced there can be a real, deep spiritual awakening in all our churches.

Two Vital Questions

What is the connection between a sweeping revival and the renewal movement—if there be any connection? That is the first vital question to be answered. It seems to me this pressing issue must be faced, especially by those who have been helped by the renewal emphasis. If renewal is of God, and I for one am fully convinced it is, despite its weaknesses, it should relate directly to the kind of awakening we need. What is the connection? I believe *renewal must in some sense be responsible for an awakening.* That answers our first question, at least in a general sense, but it also leads to another issue: *How* can renewal fulfill this responsibility? We must wait, however, to answer this central question when we put it all together in the last chapter. Now we move on to get a grip on the second great movement that is exciting the people of God today.

3
"Have You Got the Baptism, Brother?"

The door bell rang; it can't be, not this late! But it was. The day had been heavy, hurried, and harried. I had finally dropped off into a deep sleep when the bell shattered it all. I confess—which is supposed to be good for the soul—I'm not at my spiritual best when I am rudely awakened just after exhaustedly sinking into bed. But I roused out and opened the pastorium door. My feelings picked up a bit; there was an old friend from Saint Louis. He is a great guy, a layman who truly loves the Lord. With him were two men I had never met.

I urged them to come in, and we were soon sharing and rejoicing in God's blessings. My friend has a way of bringing out the best in a person. One of the other men, however, said little and kept looking at me. Quite suddenly he blurted out, "Brother, are you filled with the Holy Spirit?" I had long believed in an experience of God filling a believer with his Spirit, so I assured the good brother that I had been filled. That seemed to take him back somewhat; I really do not think he expected a firm, positive answer. There was a long pause, then he pointedly got to what he was really asking as he again inquired, "Have you had the filling with tongues?" Again I assured him God had filled me with the Spirit but that the gift of tongues was not my specific spiritual gift. I tried to tell him God had chosen to give me another ministering gift. He again paused and then urged me to seek the filling with tongues. That more or less ended that line of conversation.

I suppose most of us have had similar experiences. My new acquaintance was obviously a "charismatic." He testified to having the "baptism of the Holy Spirit," an experience that had transformed his Christian life. I imagine it probably had. It has changed lives everywhere. The charismatic approach to spirituality has become a worldwide movement with a profound impact.

What is this charismatic revival? How did it all begin? Why is there such controversy surrounding it? Why is it so aggressive? Is it actually doing good? Are Christian people genuinely helped by it? Is it of God—really? These and a thousand other questions beg for answers. To some of these issues we must address ourselves. This movement is not being "done in a corner." Persons of various denominations across the country have become involved.

History of the Charismatic Movement

To understand any contemporary movement, a grasp of its historical background is normally helpful. Yet to trace a movement which does not boast a continuous historical development is rather difficult. Such is the situation with the charismatics. This orientation to spiritual Christian living as we know it today has not always been with us. But paradoxically, the main thrust of contemporary charismatics, namely, speaking in tongues (glossolalia), has interwoven itself throughout the fabric of church history. Therefore, we shall approach the charismatic phenomenon by seeing how tongues speaking surfaced in the course of the ages.

My colleague, church historian E. Glenn Hinson, outlines the historical periodization of tongues manifestations as follows:

A.D. 100–400:   The Early Showers
A.D. 400–1500: The Long Drought
A.D. 1600–1800: The Latter Showers
1900-present: The Latter Rain [1]

I shall follow this general outline, discussing the biblical period in a different context.

The Early Showers

The turbulent four centuries from the death of the apostles through Augustine is commonly called "the age of the church fathers." These exciting days did much to forge theologies that still live. What these fathers said about the gift of tongues is therefore important. Strangely enough, however, they said very little; their references to the phenomenon are quite infrequent. The spurious ending of Mark's Gospel (16:9–16), which was probably written in the late second or early third century, has an allusion to tongues. There are a few references to glossolalia when the fathers wrote against the Montanists. Montanus, the founder of the movement, was apparently something of a charismatic. Apollonius, bishop of Tyre in the late second century, wrote that Montanus "became beside himself, and being suddenly in a sort of frenzy and ecstacy, he raved and began to babble and utter strange things, prophesying in a manner contrary to the constant custom of the church." [2] Here the brunt of the criticism is against the ecstatic nature of the prophecy, not against glossolalia per se. Irenaeus, bishop of Lyons, alluded to tongues speaking three times in his writings. The first two references are to actual languages, the last to the abuse of prophetic gifts by some who practiced the gift in an unholy way.

Perhaps the greatest of the early fathers was Tertullian. He was a Montanist himself, yet he refers to glossolalia but once in his treatise *Against Marcion*. Origen, another honored name, has only two statements about the phenomenon, and these references are rather fuzzy. He made no really clear claims. Chrysostom and Augustine both contended that they had no firsthand experience with glossolalia. Chrysostom, commenting on 1 Corinthians 12:27, went so far as to hold that tongues no longer occur. Augustine taught the same. He argued they were "signs adapted to the time" but had no contemporary relevance. And this is about all that can be found in the first four centuries of Christian theology.

The logical conclusion is that when the curtain fell on the age of the church fathers, the practice of speaking in tongues was a thing of the past in both the East and West. Hinson summarizes, "If we can trust such scanty evidence, we have to conclude that glossolalia probably occurred only intermittently and in a restricted manner in the early church. By the last quarter of the fourth century, perhaps before, it had ceased entirely." [3]

The Long Drought

If the early centuries were refreshed with only a few light showers of tongues, the next thousand years were a barren desert. About all the historians can come up with are a few names who give some sort of evidence of a glossolalia experience. For example, Gorris, in *The Christian Mystic*, labels only Anthony of Padua (1195–1231), Ange Clarenus (1300), Vincente Ferrer (1350–1419), Stephen, Colette (d.1447), John of the Cross, Francis Xavier (1506–52), Louis Bertrand (1526–81), and a few others as charismatic. The list is very meager when one realizes we are talking about 1,000 years. Furthermore, remember that the Middle Ages was a time of crass credulity and extreme mysticism. If ever the phenomenon was to occur, it seems it would have taken place in that atmosphere. Yet it did not.

The Latter Showers

The rising sun of the seventeenth century, however, burned off the medieval mists that shrouded the gift of tongues. The Reformation had broken up the monolithic, rigid structure of Roman Christianity. A new individual freedom emerged. Perhaps of even more significance, the great spiritual revival called the Puritan-pietistic movement burst on the scene. The world was open for a new rush of personal, spiritual, religious experience.

Two important outbreaks of glossolalia exploded during the seventeenth to nineteenth centuries; one was in France and the other in England. In 1685 Louis XIV revoked the Edict of Nantes which had prohibited persecution of the French Huguenots. The result was a tidal wave of fresh pressure on the Protestants, especially in southern France. Most hard hit were the Cevenal peasants—and they reacted the most. They resisted in many ways, one of which was a "spiritual" reaction; they began speaking in tongues.

The second glossolalia outbreak erupted across the English Channel among London Presbyterians. The notable and gifted pastor Edward Irving (1792–1834) became the head of a tongues movement. Irving himself never received the gift, though he sought it earnestly all of his life. Still, he was a strong advocate and popularizer of the idea. The initial impact was made in Britain when a young farm girl in Fernicarry, Scotland, broke out in glossolalia. Irving had been praying for the power of the Spirit to fall, and he saw this as an answer to his prayer. He was soon caught up in the new movement. He became so outspoken that he was tried for heresy, defrocked by the presbytery, and excommunicated from the Church of Scotland.

At the same time, glossolalia began occurring in the general revival movements of England and America. Coattailing on the surge of the awakenings mentioned in chapter 1, tongues speaking became a central phenomenon in such movements as the Ranters in the seventeenth century and the Shakers of New York and Kentucky. Even the early Quakers were anything but "quietists," as they later became known. George Fox dogmatically defended in his journal the ecstatic, spiritual experiences of his followers. It is common knowledge that the Wesleyans were profoundly shaken by unusual spiritual manifestations. John Wesley refused to condemn these aspects of the revival, though he did not overtly promote them.

The Latter Rain

As significant as these latter showers were, it was the twentieth century that brought in the flood tide of the latter rain. Why has there been a surging torrent of glossolalia in our century?

The development of contemporary tongues speaking must first be seen as a reaction to the emerging secularism of the day. Moreover, the sanctification doctrine of John Wesley had by 1867 established a firm foothold in Methodism, especially in America. Between 1880 and 1900 the Methodists split into holiness and antiholiness groups. From this historical cleavage, the Pentecostal churches eventually developed.

These Holiness churches stood on what they call the *Foursquare Gospel:* (1) entire sanctification, (2) faith healing, (3) the premillennial return of Christ, and (4) the baptism of the Holy Spirit with tongues. They saw their movement as fulfilling the prophecy of Joel 2:23 ff. concerning the "latter rain."

The rain began to fall in Topeka, Kansas, in 1901. Charles F. Parkam was the prophet who more than anyone else precipitated this new latter downpour. He was founder and leader of Bethel Bible College when the "baptism" fell. In 1906 Los Angeles had its drenching. W. J. Seymour was something of the figurehead of the cloudburst on the west coast.

From these early thunderstorms, Pentecostalism spread all over America and soon moved into Canada, Europe, and South America. For example, the Holiness movement did very well in Norway under the early leadership of T. P. Barratt of the Oslo City Mission. Pentecostal churches and denominations rapidly became worldwide.

At the midpoint of the present century, however, an unbelievable Pentecostal explosion occurred. The shock wave is still being felt here and there: not in the traditional Holiness churches alone, but all over Christendom. Tongues and other "foursquare" emphases have sent reverberations throughout all major Christian churches. Known as the "new pentecostalism," few denominations and groups have not been touched. Ecclesiastical "Richter scales" have registered the jar everywhere. The modern charismatic revival is no doubt the most startling phenomenon of the hour.

Pentecostal Inputs

Attempting to explain the neo-Pentecostal event is almost presumptuous. There have been so many different inputs which caused the flood tide that to sort them out is all but impossible. The conflict of two world wars and continual international strife, the breaking up of traditional cultures, the onrush of secularism, the inroads made by rationalistic theology, and the reaction philosophy of a pervasive existentialism all played their parts. The key, however, is probably the genuine longing of sincere Christian people to know and experience God in a personal, dynamic way. Cold orthodoxy and dead liturgy simply ran their course for many.

The Pentecostal Message

What are the neo-Pentecostals trying to say to the church in the terminal years of this tempestuous twentieth century? They are surely saying something; no movement has been more militantly missionary.

First, "total sanctification" is usually stressed, though admittedly not always. Wesley, who is probably responsible for this emphasis, asked:

Whom then do you mean by "one that is sanctified"? We mean one in "whom is the mind which was in Christ," and who so "walketh as Christ also walked"; a man "that hath clean hands and a pure heart," or that is "cleansed from all filthiness of flesh and spirit": one in whom is "no occasion of stumbling," and who accordingly "does not commit sin." To declare this a little more particularly: We understand by that scriptural expression, "a perfect man," one in whom God hath fulfilled His faithful word, "From all your filthiness and from all your idols I will cleanse you: I will also save you from all your uncleanness." We understand hereby, one whom God hath "sanctified throughout, in body, soul, and spirit," and one who "walketh in the light as He is in the light; in whom is no darkness at all: the blood of Jesus Christ His Son having cleansed him from all sin."

This man can now testify to all mankind, "I am crucified with Christ: nevertheless I live; yet not I, but Christ liveth in me." He is "holy as God who called him is holy," both in heart and "in all manner of conversation." He "loveth the Lord his God with all his heart," and serveth Him with "all his strength." He "loveth his neighbour," every man, "as himself"; yea, "as Christ loveth us"; them in particular that despitefully use him, and persecute him, because they know not the Son, neither the Father. Indeed his soul is all love; filled with "bowels of mercies, kindness, meekness, gentleness, long-suffering." And his life agreeth thereto, full of "the work of faith, the patience of hope, the labour of love." "And whatsoever he doeth, either in word or deed, he doeth it all in the name," in the love and power, "of the Lord Jesus." In a word, he doeth "the will of God on earth, as it is done in heaven." [4]

The degree to which neo-Pentecostals push this line varies. Some believe they have had an experience that completely eradicates the sinful tendency of the heart. Others reject any sort of perfectionism, stressing only the necessity of continual confession on the basis of 1 John 1:9. Most of us have met both kinds. I well remember my first real encounter with a hard-core perfectionist. I was a very young Christian stationed in Japan as a soldier in 1946. The perfectionist I met told me personal sin was no problem to him; he had been totally perfected and was above it all. On the other hand, some charismatics openly confess they sin and need constant cleansing. Views on sanctification seem to vary as to how serious one takes his respective Arminian or Cal-

vinistic backgrounds. Regardless, some form of perfectionism has always cut out its niche in Pentecostalism.

Faith Healing

The second cornerstone of the Foursquare Gospel concerns itself with faith healing. This idea is also something
of a mixed bag with neo-Pentecostals. Few, if any, deny
the power of God to heal, but some obviously engage in
faith healing activities far more than others. Practices range
all the way from simply praying for the sick to the dogmatic
assertion that God will heal anyone if the person has enough
faith—and then they usually go about seeking to conjure
it all up. It must be granted, however, that a maturity is
seemingly developing in this aspect of the movement. A
case in point is the ministry of Oral Roberts. I heard him
while I was a seminary student. He preached under a huge
tent. At that time he conducted the traditional Pentecostal
healing line service. Today, as most are aware, Roberts is
building a 100-million-dollar medical-dental school at Oral
Roberts University. This is quite a shift from his early ministry.

Premillennialism

Thirdly, the premillennial return of Christ has always
been a bedrock emphasis in mainline Pentecostal churches.
But since the neo-Pentecostals burst on the scene, the new
believers have tended to bring their eschatological baggage
with them. Although major Pentecostal denominations have
been dispensational and premillennial, as has traditional fundamentalism, the neo-Pentecostals generally retain the prophetic framework with which they were brought up.

The Baptism in the Holy Spirit

Finally, but very far from least, the baptism in the Holy
Spirit is stressed. This is actually the central thrust of the

movement. Although it is perhaps unfair to generalize, several ideas appear to be widely accepted. First, the baptism in the Holy Spirit is an experience to be distinguished from conversion. Most Pentecostals want new believers led into the experience commensurate with conversion, but they feel most Christians have had little or no experience of the Holy Spirit in their daily lives. Thus they tend to precipitate a post-conversion crisis that will bring the believer to an infilling of the Spirit, attested to by glossolalia.

When the movement was young and more aligned with traditional Pentecostalism, it was all but unanimously agreed that the final test of the validity of the baptism experience was speaking in tongues. This is probably why the movement became known as the glossolalia movement. There has been some moving away from this rigid stance in recent times however. It seems the movement is beginning to realize that the Spirit may impart other gifts and that one can be Spirit-filled and not necessarily speak in tongues. Yet this is a quite recent concession and far from being universally accepted.

Further, there is a wide divergence of opinion as to the effects of the baptism in the Holy Spirit. Some are rigid perfectionists and equate the baptism with a move into entire sanctification as discussed earlier. Others see it merely as a means of praise and personal blessing. About the only unanimity is the agreement that it imparts great power, liberates the believers for service, and makes Christ a dynamic, present reality. Nonetheless, the Holy Spirit baptism emphasis is what binds the whole movement together and gives it the general spirit of unity it seems to enjoy.

Now we would all surely agree that the Holy Spirit works to develop a deep spiritual quality in our daily Christian walk. And we all must grant, it seems to me, that many believers have been genuinely helped by the glossolalia emphasis. I for one do not feel the movement can be simply and summarily written off as some like to do. God has done a real work in many lives. This is self-evident. Yet there are serious problems.

Some Problems to Face

I confess I have definite difficulties with neo-Pentecostalism. The first is doctrinal deviation, at least as I see it. For example, although the Bible has much to say to believers about "walking in the Spirit" (Gal. 5:16), being "filled with the Spirit" (Eph. 5:18), bearing the fruit of the Spirit (Gal. 5:22–25), the "baptism of the Spirit" is *always* presented in the Bible as a synonym for conversion. *All* saved people are baptized by the Spirit into the body of Christ (1 Cor. 12:13). After conversion, one should surely be continually filled with the Spirit and bear fruit. About that there is no argument. But the baptism and being born again are one and the same.

Furthermore, to equate the Holy Spirit's infilling and the gift of tongues, as is so often done, is very dubious indeed. The stress of the Scriptures on the Spirit's fullness has to do with ethics and morality. The *fruit* of the Spirit, not a *gift* of the Spirit, is the true test of God's infilling (Eph. 3:17–19). There can be little doubt about this fact when one honestly and objectively interprets the relevant biblical passages on the work of the Holy Spirit. The relationship of the Spirit to the so-called gifts revolves around the idea that God imparts gifts as spiritual ministries with which one is to serve Jesus Christ. The gifts make one Christlike in service. The fruit of the Spirit makes one Christlike in character. That is why Paul called love, the fruit, the higher way (1 Cor. 12:31).

The Issue

There are several other practices and concepts held by Pentecostals that perhaps should be discussed: their inordinate quest to lead others into the glossolalia experience, their often-found exclusiveness, and their excessive emotionalism.

Yet my biggest problem with neo-Pentecostalism is the same as that with the renewal emphasis. It tends to turn in on itself, get extremely missionary about enlisting others into its own unique group, and never truly transforms the whole body of Christ. This problem has been so serious that it has at times caused ruinous ruptures in relationships, even splits in churches, although I will grant that error can usually be found on both sides of such schisms.

The Great Need

Therefore, as deeply as I appreciate what God has done in many lives through the glossolalia movement, again I must ask: Why has it not revived the mainstream of most churches? Why has it not been the catalyst for the kind of awakening we need? This is the issue that the neo-Pentecostals must face—just as the renewal movement must. But again we forebear seeking an answer to the most crucial issue as we move on to a consideration of the third great movement that has had impact on the church today.

4
Filled, Satisfied, Victorious, and Useful

I never heard anyone pray like that before! That thought bounced around in my mind as the man prayed on. We were standing in sawdust under the roof of a little open-air tabernacle. A layman had purchased three lots, built a roof shelter, scattered sawdust on the ground, called it The Baptist Tabernacle, and asked me to start preaching. We were to begin services the next Sunday, and we were asking God to bless this new work. I knew the layman who started it all very well, but this fellow was praying in a manner I had never experienced. Actually, I decided he either knew God in a way I didn't or he was a religious nut. I soon learned the former was right; he really knew God.

To make a very long story short, this man led me into a body of biblical truth that radically rerouted the course of my ministry. He told me he had come into a deep experience of God through the message of the Keswick Movement. This approach to spiritual Christian living had its early beginnings over one hundred years ago in England through the ministry of some visiting Americans. It came back to the United States in force under such titles as the deeper life, the Spirit-filled life, the victorious life, and the abundant life. Many know it as the Keswick message, and many have been significantly and profoundly deepened in the Spirit through its worldwide thrust.

The History of Keswick

In the early 1870s England experienced several powerful spiritual influences at work. The Church of England began to come alive, even though the emphases varied. The high church element was agitating for new life to eliminate the general unconcern of Christians. Many leaders had been significantly deepened by the Oxford movement. The middle party of the Anglican Church was contending for more involvement in social issues. The low church Evangelicals, strongly influenced by Methodism, were constantly on the quest for simplicity of worship and the necessity of a genuine conversion experience.

The so-called "dissenting churches," the Plymouth Brethren in particular, were becoming increasingly influential. With a strong Calvinistic emphasis on obedience to the Word of God, they widely stimulated diligent Bible study and a radical return to the simplicity of the Christian experience. Brethren influence was tremendous, extending far beyond their own denominational borders.

Further, the evangelistic ministry of D. L. Moody and Ira Sankey shook the British Isles in 1873–74. In the leading metropolitan areas of Britain the response to Moody's preaching was all but overwhelming. Thousands were converted and tens of thousands deepened.

Influences from the United States had not only come via the Moody-Sankey campaigns, but the American "Higher Life" teaching was invading the old country also. In 1859 W. E. Boardman published his devotional classic, *The Higher Christian Life.* Pearse says this book was "perhaps the first treatise on this subject that won its popular way among all denominations; and its vast circulation both in America and England, not only melted the prejudices of hosts against this subject, but made it possible for other writers to follow in the paths which he had opened, and let multitudes of timid souls out of the misty dawn into the clear shining of the sun." [1]

Other influential books began bombarding Britain. Then Mr. and Mrs. Robert Pearsall Smith exploded on the Christian scene. Born in Philadelphia they became dedicated Quakers. In the Smiths' early Christian experiences, although they knew the joy of forgiveness of sins, they experienced little deliverance from sin's power. Deeply burdened, they began to cry as Paul had, "O wretched man that I am! who shall deliver me from the body of this death?" (Rom. 7:24). They said they knew of justification by faith but nothing of sanctification by faith. So the Smiths simply struggled on.

Sanctification by Faith

In 1867 Mrs. Smith came to the tremendous truth that it is faith, not struggling, that brings daily victory over the power of sin. God spoke the principle to her through a young Baptist theological student and a lay Methodist dressmaker. At first her husband thought she was being led into error, but he too soon came to the same place of personal victory by faith. It turned their lives around.

Both the Smiths were gifted writers and speakers. Despite the fact that they were not theologically trained, they were soon in constant demand for spiritual life conferences. Their message began to captivate the mind-set of Christians everywhere. Invitations poured in. Smith's strenuous speaking schedule, in addition to his on-going business affairs, soon took its toll on his health. To rest and recuperate the Smiths traveled to England in 1872. There invitations to hold meetings poured in on them and they responded. In the course of only a few months over two thousand ministers had heard their message. One of those who embraced the Higher Life, as it came to be called, was the Reverend Evan H. Hopkins. He was destined to be the leader and spokesman in early days of the Keswick Movement.

A Growing Movement

In the summer of 1874, Lord Mount Temple, at the urging of a number of university men from Cambridge, called a six-day Christian life conference at "Broadlands," the residence of Lord Palmerston. One hundred attended and all were deeply moved. Another conference was proposed on a much larger scale. Sir Arthur Blackwood, head of the British Post Office, suggested it be held in Oxford in early autumn. Large numbers came, even from the Continent. The principal speakers were Robert Pearsall Smith, the Reverend Evan H. Hopkins, and American Higher Life leaders Asa Nahan and W. E. Boardman.

One of those attending the Oxford Convention was the Reverend Canon T. D. Harford-Battersly, Vicar of Saint John's Anglican Church in Keswick, a small town in northern England's beautiful Lake District. He was radically renewed by the Oxford experience. Here is his own testimony: "I got a revelation of Christ to my soul, so extraordinary, glorious, and precious, that from that day it illuminated my life. I found *He* was *all* I wanted; I shall never forget it; the day and hour are present with me. How it humbled me and yet what peace it brought." [2] The Keswick Convention was about to be born.

The Brighton Meeting

Within nine months of the great Oxford Convention, an even larger group attended a series of Higher Life meetings held in Brighton on England's south coast. Thousands came. D. L. Moody was just closing his London campaign in the famous Covent Garden as the Brighton Convention opened. He sent the following telegram to those assembled in Brighton: "Moody and 8,000 persons at the closing meeting at the Opera House have specially prayed for the Convention, that great results may follow." God answered; so great was the attendance that three huge halls had to be utilized, and the blessings paralleled the attendance. Countless Christian lives were wonderfully transformed.

The First Keswick Convention

At the Brighton Convention, Canon Harford-Battersly and a Quaker friend, Robert Wilson, decided to hold a similar convention at Keswick. They invited Mr. and Mrs. Pearsall

Smith with Mr. Smith as the presider. The meetings were to begin on June 29, just three weeks after the closing of the Brighton meeting.

Then everything seemed to fall apart. The Smiths suddenly announced they were returning to America—his health had deteriorated, they said. Other speakers also withdrew. But Harford-Battersly and Wilson carried on, rented a tent to seat 400, and had good blessings.

The Smiths returned to America under a dark cloud of suspicion concerning doctrinal heresy. Tragically the rumors mounted until the whole Higher Life movement was called in question. Yet Harford-Battersly and Wilson were convinced of the truth of the Higher Life approach and called for another conference in Keswick the next spring. There could be no retreat; they were assured God was in the matter. This time great crowds attended and blessings abounded. The die was cast. As one historian has put it: "After that there was never any doubt that it should be held yearly. Since then it has grown year by year, until now those who attend, coming from many parts of the world, number in the thousands." [3] I have sat under the tent in Keswick myself, and it is all that has been said about it. Deep blessings do abound among the thousands who attend every summer in the beautiful little village in the lovely Lake District.

Since the early uneasy days, the Keswick Movement has spread world wide. Few in the evangelical world, whether realizing it or not, have failed to be influenced by the emphasis. Keswick is responsible for popularizing Bible conferences in Britain and to some extent significantly changed the camp meeting method in America. The giants who have come out of the thrust are legendary: F. B. Meyer, Andrew Murray, G. Campbell Morgan, A. T. Pierson, R. A. Torrey, contemporaries like John Stott, Stephen Olford, and a host of others. I confess that men like these and their understanding of the spiritual Christian experience have been profoundly significant in my life and ministry.

Now let's turn to what these Keswick thinkers are trying to say to the church.

Keswick Concepts

A definite sequence of ideas emerges in a typical Keswick convention, whether in England or elsewhere. It takes the motif of a spiritual clinic. Most Christian people are carnal—spiritually sick. They need to go through an extensive examination, be diagnosed, given the prescription, and set on the road to health. The convention begins with an in-depth diagnosis of the illness.

The Exceeding Sinfulness of Sin

"In a clinic, the first need is accurate diagnosis . . . therefore . . . the first aim is the discovery and acknowledgement of the sin that doth so easily beset us," [4] so speaks a Keswick preacher. That strikes the first anvil blow, the exceeding sinfulness of sin.

Keswick is convinced that the fatal flaw of the faithful, that which consequently diverts the missionary ministry of God's people, is a defective view of sin. What is sin? they ask. Evan Hopkins gives the most decisive definition in his classic *The Law of Liberty in the Spiritual Life.* He first tells us what sin is *not.* Man's rebellion, he states, is not "an inseparable adjunct to our human nature." [5] Man was not originally created with this flaw; sin is not "a necessary constituent of our moral progress." [6] We are not compelled to sin.

Hopkins then positively points out the six segments of sin in the saints.[7]

1. Sin is an offense against God. The fact of Christ's death shows what an awful offense against God sin actually is. The horror of this offense is pointed up in the fact that sin breaks fellowship with God and that it took Christ's atoning death to heal the breach.

2. Sin is not mere outward acts, rather it "includes all those *inner* activities of the soul which are opposed to the mind and character of God." [8] Sin is a *power.* Moreover, it has invaded every vestige of human experience. Paul's cry of despair in Romans 7:24, "O wretched man that I am . . . ," shows us that apart from Christ, sin rules in the heart.

3. Sin is moral defilement. Sin is the antithesis of holiness, the essence of God's nature. Thus we become unclean and unfit for the presence of a holy God when we sin. After a glimpse of God and his consuming holiness, the sinner is overwhelmed with a sense of his personal guilt. He falls before God as Isaiah and cries out, "Woe is me! for I am undone . . . I am a man of unclean lips" (Isa. 6:5). As Lady MacBeth lamented, "All the perfumes of Arabia will not sweeten this little hand."

4. Sin is a spiritual disease. "Sin is to the soul what disease is to the body. The effect of disease on our physical organism is just a picture of what sin produces in our spiritual nature." [9] The Lord's physical healings while on earth are illustrations of what he can do spiritually. Sin is always active—eating away at the vitals of all who disobey. This devastating effect of sin makes even God's children dull of hearing and slow to obey. This fact is not often honestly faced by Christians.

5. Sin is an acquired habit. We are not born with evil habits; they are learned. Keswick is not Augustinian in its view of the fallen nature—and that to its credit. Although we all have a tendency to sin, there is a difference between inherent tendencies and acquired habits. Furthermore, the so-called respectable sins such as worry, bad temper, and the like are as heinous in the sight of a holy God as the overt sins of the flesh.

6. Sin is an indwelling tendency. The "law of sin" (Rom.

7:23, 25; 8:2) is always with us. This law, as Keswick
sees it, is as fixed and unbending as the physical laws
that govern the universe. Some Holiness groups teach
that one can escape this law, but this is a perversion
not only of Scriptures (1 John 1:8, 10) but also of
experience. Purity can become a *maintained condition;* there is victory in Christ, but it can never become a *state* in this life.

It must be remembered that Keswick sermons on sin
are directed to the saints, not sinners. Nor is the intent of
such messages to present theological discourses on the nature of sin. The speakers take the stand of the Old Testament
prophets in their preaching to Israel: the fearless pointing
out of sin in God's people and the call to repentance. Andrew
Murray said, "The block in the advancement of Christ's kingdom today is not on account of the circumstances or the
special difficulties of our age, but the block is found in the
Church itself." [10] Saints need to be shocked into the reality
of the seriousness of their sin. The constant cry of Christians
should be that of the psalmist, "Search me, O God, and
know my heart; try me; and know my thoughts; And see
if there be any wicked way in me, and lead me in the way
everlasting" (Ps. 139:23–24). Believers must realize sin is
loathsome, heinous, exceedingly sinful. All this may sound
negative, but the realization of sin is where Christian maturity begins. Without this painful diagnosis there is no spirituality. This is Keswick's starting point.

Carnal Christians

The sin problem is acute because Christians are immature, carnal. The carnal Christian has four characteristics,
we are told. One, a state of protracted infancy in Christ
persists. Although spiritual immaturity is a natural state immediately after conversion, it should not continue. There
are two marks of "spiritual babyhood": (1) infant Christians

cannot help themselves, and (2) they cannot help others. Some believers have been like this all their believing lives. Secondly, carnality is a state in which sin is supreme. The Corinthian church is a classic example of this with its divisions, envyings, and immorality. Thirdly, the carnal state can coexist with great spiritual gifts. People can serve fervently and effectively and yet be carnal. In a word, one can exercise his gifts of the Spirit and be almost devoid of the fruit of the Spirit. Again, Corinth is pointed out as an example. In the fourth place, immaturity sidetracks the receiving of spiritual truth. Baby believers can easily fall into the trap James urged Christians to avoid, being hearers only and not doers of the word (Jas. 1:22).

All of this, Hopkins points out, makes believers (1) satisfied with partial truth, (2) satisfied with partial consecration, (3) satisfied with partial obedience, and (4) satisfied with partial love. A Christian, content with incomplete spirituality, will soon become an entire worldling. That is tragic—so commonly tragic.

It must be realized that God is deeply involved with the controversy his people have with him over sin. God is *shocked* at the sin Christians take for granted, and the saints should be shocked, too. As Cardinal Newman once said, "The one great security against sin (is) to be shocked by it." [11]

It is right here that the Holy Spirit does his beautiful sanctifying work. God's Spirit not only reveals sin but he also works to sever the saints from their sins. His cleansing work is as thorough as his revealing work. God will not leave us to stew in the sin situation if we long for deliverance. God provides a way out. There is sanctification and victory for the believer. This is Keswick's next step.

God's Provision for Sin: Sanctification and Victory

The reason Christians seem to fail so often is because of God's high ethical standards. The conditions for consecrated Christian character are clear: we are to love our enemies (Matt. 5:44); to give thanks in *all* things (Eph. 5:20); to worry about nothing (Phil. 4:6–7); to rejoice always (Phil. 4:4); to be blameless and without rebuke (Phil. 2:15); to walk as Jesus walked (1 John 2:6); and to be overcomers (Rom. 8:37). Little wonder we have difficulty in living like that! Is it even thinkable to attempt to advance such a standard? The Bible tells us we must. Keswick tells us we can. There is no place in the Scriptures that even implies that we cannot attain God's ideal.

Yet it is clear that defeat and depression dog the heels of many believers. We seem to fail continually and grow so little. Our experience is often like that which Hudson Taylor expressed in a letter written to his sister three years after he founded the great China Inland Mission.

I prayed, agonized, fasted, strove, made resolutions, read the Word more diligently, sought more time for meditation but all without avail. Everyday, almost every hour, the consciousness of sin oppressed me. I knew that if only I could abide in Christ all would be well, but I could not. . . . Is there no rescue? Must it be thus to the end—constant conflict, and too often defeat? [12]

Learning to Cope

Learning to cope with sin is the issue. Keswick speakers begin by exposing false ways of dealing with the problem in the Christian life. First they tell us the Spirit's sanctification never "just happens." Therefore, Christians cannot be casual. Nor is sanctification a matter of gradual growth that the believers can neither impede or hasten. This does not mean that spirituality and Christian victory are not maturing experiences; they surely are. But God's people must do something about them.

Furthermore, hoping for eradication of the sin principle in one's life is a fantasy. The Bible and personal experience both make this plain. But the constant attempt to suppress the "old man" is no answer either. Paul learned that. He said,

For that which I do I allow not: for what I would, that do I not; but what I hate, that do I. For I know that in me (that is, in my flesh) dwelleth no good thing: for to will is present with me; but how to perform that which is good I find not. For the good that I would I do not: but the evil which I would not, that I do (Rom. 7:15, 18–19).

Whether Paul was speaking of his pre- or post-conversion experience is not the point. The attempt to sail in the flesh against sin's fierce storm will always send one down. Here are the rocks where the vast majority of believers have run aground. Even much of the preaching heard in pulpits today is no more than admonitions, such as: don't do this, don't do that, don't do the other thing, with little help offered on *how* not to do them. About all this kind of preaching accomplishes is to give sensitive people a guilt trip. You cannot sanctify the flesh by the flesh. So our dear people struggle on. Is there a solution? Should we forget it all and just plug along? Never, cries Keswick!

What then is the answer? Here Keswick makes a most significant contribution. Although some condemn the movement as negative and always dwelling on sin, this really isn't true. The emphasis is positive; one of its main thrusts is the glorious news that in Jesus Christ there is victory. The only reason for raising the sin issue is to bring believers to the reality of sin's sinfulness and how marvelous it is to live as "more than conquerors through him who loved us" (Rom. 8:37). God makes provision. What then is the message? It is sanctification *by faith*.

Sanctification by Faith, Not Works

Sanctification, growth in Christ and victory over sin, is viewed in a three-sided frame. First, there is *positional sanctification*. In Christ we are already perfect because of our unity with the Lord Jesus. Every believer shares in this. Secondly, *ultimate sanctification* comes at the Lord's return. All true believers take part in this resurrection to fullness of life. Thirdly, *experiential sanctification* is the down-to-earth, everyday work of the Holy Spirit where positional sanctification becomes a practical, experiential reality. All believers do not necessarily share in this side of sanctification. Therefore, it is with this aspect of the Spirit's work we are most vitally concerned.

Experiential sanctification is likewise wrapped up in a threefold frame: a process, a crisis, and a gift. The third aspect, sanctification as a gift, is the core of Keswick teaching. All realize salvation is a gift of God's grace (Rom. 6:23). Few understand sanctification is also of grace. In other words, we do not move from the faith principle for salvation to the works of the law for sanctification. Christ must be accepted as our sanctification as well as our righteousness. Paul said, "He is made unto us wisdom, and righteousness, *and sanctification"* (1 Cor. 1:30 author's italics). The gift of holiness must be worked out in our daily lives, but we work from holiness, not to holiness. Sanctification is a gift of grace every bit as much as salvation. But how does one implement this principle in practical Christian living?

The Believer's Identification with Christ

The first truth to be grasped is that Christ's death is sufficient not only for *sin* (as a principle) but also for *sins* (particular failures). Secondly, all that Calvary implies must be appropriated *by faith*. As John put it, "This is the victory that overcomes the world, our faith" (1 John 5:4, RSV). Paul stated, "For therein is the righteousness of God revealed from faith to faith: as it is written, The just shall live by faith" (Rom. 1:17). In the letter to his sister, Hudson Taylor went on to say, "gradually light dawned, I saw that faith was the only requisite—was the hand to lay hold on his fulness and make it mine."

Yet faith must have an object. It will not do to say to the despairing Christian, "Have faith, Brother," and simply leave him there. In what truth then are we to have faith so as to overcome the power of our sins? Paul told us:

What shall we say then? Shall we continue in sin, that grace may abound? God forbid. How shall we, that are dead to sin, live any longer therein? Know ye not, that so many of us as were baptized into Jesus Christ were baptized into his death? Therefore we are buried with him by baptism into death: that like as Christ was raised up from the dead by the glory of the Father, even so we also should walk in newness of life. For if we have been planted together in the likeness of his death, we shall be also in the likeness of his resurrection: Knowing this, that our old man is crucified with him, that the body of sin might be destroyed, that henceforth we should not serve sin. For he that is dead is freed from sin. Now if we be dead with Christ, we believe that we shall also live with him: knowing that Christ being raised from the dead dieth no more; death hath no more dominion over him. For in that he died, he died unto sin once: but in that he liveth, he liveth unto God. Likewise reckon ye also yourselves to be dead indeed unto sin, but alive unto God through Jesus Christ our Lord. Let not sin therefore reign in your mortal body, that ye should obey it in the lusts thereof. Neither yield ye your members as instruments of unrighteousness unto sin: but yield yourselves unto God, as those that are alive from the dead, and your members as instruments of righteousness unto God. For sin shall not have dominion over you: for ye are not under the law, but under grace (Rom. 6:1–14).

Here is the prime point. When Christ died on the cross for sin, we were identified with him in that death. *We died with him.* Furthermore, when he arose, we were resurrected also. By our union with him in his death and resurrection, we are not only freed from the judgment of our evil but we are also set free from its power. We really are dead to sin in Christ and alive to God in resurrection. Therefore, we claim that position in Christ by faith just as we claim forgiveness and salvation by faith in Christ's work.

All this is most difficult to grasp rationally. It appeals primarily to faith. The rationale, at least as far as it can be understood, centers in Paul's favorite phrase: *in Christ.* Paul used this expression or its equivalent over 160 times in his New Testament letters. It means literally "in union with Christ." James Stewart states that to fail to realize what Paul meant by "in Christ" is to fail to understand Paul's grasp of Christianity. It has the impact that we are so intrinsically united with Christ by faith that when he died on the cross we died too; when he arose, we also shared in his resurrection.

Thus we find ourselves as much in Christ as he is in us. But to know this is not enough; we must enter it by faith. Faith appropriates the reality of our position in Christ. Deliverance from the power of sin, therefore, is no more a human attainment than salvation is an accomplishment of the flesh. It is a gift of God's grace. We simply claim the victory by faith because we are dead to sin.

Keswick calls this truth the Magna Charta of the Christian. Here we are set at liberty. Although the "law of sin and death" is always present, "the law of the Spirit of life in Christ Jesus" is greater (Rom. 8:1). The new law sets us free from the old. The old is counteracted through faith.

Does this eliminate spiritual warfare? Of course not! But it is not a battle of the flesh against the flesh. It is the battle of faith. The warfare is to stay on the ground of faith where victory is found; that is the battle. Of course, the appropriation of faith is not always easy. For some reason we seem to find it difficult to give up our human strivings and simply claim all of God's blessing by faith. As Barabas expresses it:

It is necessary that the Christian prepare himself for the conflict. He must be strong in the Lord, and in the power of His might (Eph. 6:10). For this he must first clearly see the nature of the victory Christ has obtained for His people. At Calvary, He vanquished all spiritual adversaries. The next step is to identify himself with Christ in His victory. He must *by faith plant his feet on the victorious position Christ obtained for him.* . . . That at once, shows the nature of the fight; he fights not in order to reach the place of victory, but; occupying the position already obtained for him by Christ, he fights from it.[13]

All of this assumes that the believer deeply desires victory and is yielded to God in every aspect of life. But when it all comes together one can fight the spiritual battle with the expectations of victory. That is good news indeed!

Consecration

If dedication to the absolute will of God is presupposed in all that has been said concerning spiritual victory, can it be assumed that all Christians are to that place of surrender? Obviously not! Commitment thus surfaces as a central theme of the movement.

Consecration to God's will demands two vital exercises. First of all, sins must be individually confessed. Sin as a principle was defeated in conversion, but daily specific sins must be brought specifically before God in confession. One by one, individual sins must be acknowledged before God, claiming the promise of 1 John 1:9: "If we confess our sins, he is faithful and just to forgive us our sins, and to cleanse us from all unrighteousness." As a contemporary Keswick-type speaker has put it, "We need to get all our sins confessed up-to-date." When we get honest and objective about sins, forgiveness and cleansing come.

In the second place, one must be completely yielded to the will of God. Here Keswick really zeroes in on the believer. The question is raised, Is consecration a crisis or a process? Does it occur in one great act of dedication to God or is it a continual process? Keswick is quick to answer that it is both-and, not either-or. These statements are frequently heard: "Sanctification is a process beginning with a crisis," and "Sanctification is a crisis with a view to a process."

The existential consecration crisis Keswick seeks to foster is usually precipitated because of the need of a radical updating of one's original surrender of repentance at conversion. It means bringing all of one's self to the absolute authority of Jesus Christ. As the Keswick poet Theodore Monod expressed it:

> Oh, the bitter shame and sorrow,
>   That a time could ever be,
> When I let the Savior's pity
> Plead in vain, and proudly say,
>   "All of self and none of Thee."
>
> Yet He found me; I beheld Him
>   Bleeding on the accursed tree;
> Heard Him pray, "Forgive them, Father,"
> And my wistful heart said faintly,
>   "Some of self, and some of Thee."
>
> Day by day His tender mercy,
>   Healing, helping, full and free,
> Sweet and strong, and ah! so patient,
> Brought me lower while I whispered,
>   "Less of self, and more of Thee."
>
> Higher than the highest heavens,
>   Deeper than the deepest sea,
> Lord, thy love at last hath conquered:
> Grant me now my soul's petition,
>   "None of self, and all of Thee." [14]

The continual process centers in discovering more areas of life that must be brought under Christ's control. Through study, experience, and walking with Christ, new aspects of life where Christ has not been given lordship are revealed. Then because of the crisis of absolute committal, the consecrated Christian brings that new area under Christ's authority. It starts with a big *yes* to God's will and continues with a lifelong series of affirmations.

This new attitude of surrender sweeps away all barriers between the believer and God. Now the way is open for the fullness of God's blessings.

The Spirit-Filled Life

The Keswick Movement is first and foremost a Spirit-filled life movement. It is to this goal that the entire thrust moves. The Holy Spirit is to be to us today all that Jesus was to his disciples in their day. As the Spirit of truth, the Holy Spirit leads into all truth; as Comforter he is available in every trial; as Teacher he will guide one to know how to be pleasing to God.

Yet it is clear that not many Christians experience the Holy Spirit in such a fashion. The carnality and self-centered life that characterizes many believers is ample evidence. What is seen in many individual lives also show up in the church as a whole. Where is the power, winsomeness, and warmth that should characterize the body of Christ? A mighty move of the Spirit is the great need in most congregations.

This certainly does not mean Christians are completely devoid of the Spirit. To the contrary; all true believers possess the Holy Spirit (Rom. 8:9). But all Christians are obviously not *filled* with the Spirit. The principle is so central to Keswick teaching that "it is largely true to say that it was a recognition of this fact on the part of Christian people that brought the Keswick Convention into being." [15] Why this insistence on a Spirit-filled experience?

First, it is the clear teaching of the Scriptures. The early disciples were filled with the Holy Spirit (Acts 2:4; 4:31). Contemporary Christians are commanded to be filled with the Spirit (Eph. 5:18), walk in the Spirit (Gal. 5:16), mortify the deeds of the body through the Spirit (Rom. 8:13), grieve not the Spirit (Eph. 4:30), quench not the Spirit (1 Thess. 5:19), and be led by the Spirit (Rom. 8:14). In a word, Christians are to have welling up from their innermost being the "rivers of living waters" of the Holy Spirit (John 7:38).

Secondly, this quality of Christianity makes believers a blessing to others. Andrew Murray expressed it this way, "The fullness of the Spirit is simply the full preparation for living and working as a Child of God." [16] Moreover, Keswick often makes a distinction between "full" and "filled" with the Spirit. The first implies an abiding habitual state, the latter denotes a special anointing for some special service on some special occasion. Evan Hopkins, Bishop Handley Moule, G. Campbell Morgan, and others have drawn this line of distinction. Morgan said, "What is needed for life is the perpetual filling of the Spirit which is the normal condition of those who are living in the way of God, and the specific fillings to overflowing which may always be counted on when special service demands." [17]

How Fullness Comes

How, then, is one filled with the Spirit? This is the central question and challenge. Keswick tells us that the reception of this fullness of the Spirit is a *definite act of faith* separable from regeneration, but not necessarily separated from it in time. There is no need for any time lapse between receiving the Spirit at conversion (1 Cor. 12:13) and appropriating the fullness of the Spirit for sanctification, power in service, and fruit-bearing. The problem is, few new believers are led into this truth at the time of their conversion. Hence a time lapse occurs. Why not lead converts into all God has for them? Christians surely did in the first century (Acts 2:38). As a person accepts Christ by faith, he can also accept the fullness of God's Spirit by faith.

Yet it must be clearly understood that the infilling is not a once-for-all experience. It is a walk, a constant act of faith, a continual spirit of confession and consecration. Is it a second blessing? Yes, but it is also a third, fourth, hundredth, and thousandth blessing. The Holy Spirit continually fills one as needs arise.

A Practical Guide

Five principles to God's fullness are usually outlined. They can be expressed as follows.

> *Acknowledge*—your need
> *Abandon*—your sin
> *Abdicate*—your heart's throne to Christ

Ask—in faith

Accept—it as a completed act

This outline should not be understood in a legalistic sense; it is merely a guide to describe a walk of dedication and faith. Most important, this blessing is not for super-Christians alone. All believers can share in the experience. Christians who are not filled with the Spirit actually sin, for God has commanded that they be filled with the Spirit. They sin against God, a needy world, and themselves. They rob their whole sphere of influence of God's blessings if they fail to walk in the Spirit's fullness.

What are the results of being filled with the Spirit? Blessings incalculable for oneself and others! W. Graham Scroggie put it this way: "If we have the fullness of the Spirit, we should be at *rest*. Feverish service will be at an end. Not that we will cease to work, but there will be rest in work, so that we may accomplish even incredible things quietly and restfully. Then we shall have *joy*, for 'the fruit of the Spirit is joy.' This joy will be beyond the reach of circumstances and is obvious. Another product is *love*, for the Lord and his people. 'The fruit of the Spirit is love.' There will be *power* in Christian work, in secular work—wherever the Lord has put us, and then there will be victory—consistent victory—over sin." [18]

In other words, the purpose of the Spirit's fullness is powerful Christian service. The fullness of joy is not the end. Honoring God in a powerful ministry is the goal. God fills us to bless others. It makes us witnesses. Evangelism comes to the fore. "The chief end of man is to glorify God and enjoy him forever."

The Strength of Keswick

It has probably become very clear that of the three movements discussed, the Keswick approach appeals to me the most. There are several reasons. In the first place, in my view, it is by far the most scriptural. It avoids the errors of perfectionism, glossolalia, and other such pitfalls. Secondly, it is usually not as "turned in on itself" as the other movements tend to be. Thirdly, Keswick goes much deeper and sidesteps some of the psychological and emotional excesses of the others. Finally, when a true awakening occurs, history shows us (as we shall later see) that the theological and experiential aspects of the awakening go along Keswick lines—hence its relevance and impact.

Ever since that prayer meeting in our little tabernacle many years ago that introduced me to the deeper life movement, I have been preaching that message. I have seen many lives transformed, deepened, and blessed.

The Big Problem Surfaces Again

One thing deeply disturbs me about the Keswick movement however. I have been forced to conclude, along with the renewal and charismatic movements, Keswick has touched only the hungry few. Despite its strength and worldwide influence, Keswick has not moved the mainstream of the church. The average congregation still flows along in its river of mediocrity and lethargy. Keswick simply has not transformed and revived the entire church of God. Where, oh, where is the revival we need? Will the awakening that must come ever dawn?

5
Born in Revival

Why all this urgency for a fresh awakening? Isn't it enough to be content with what is happening? Why the concern? Are not the current renewal movements revitalizing the churches in significant segments? Even if the bulk of believers are seemingly untouched, hasn't God always worked through the faithful remnant? Do we actually need a repeat of the past?

Well, thank God for what is happening, yet it is evident that what is occurring in the kingdom is *simply not enough.* We need a fresh awakening, first of all, because God has always given these blessed full showers when the church found itself in crisis. That we face a crisis today is obvious. The breakdown of morality, the onrush of the secular society, the alarming apathy of the church, and a thousand other factors all cry for an awakening. These issues surely create the atmosphere for a revival.

Further, if we are earnest about world evangelization, if we take the Great Commission seriously, an awakening is vital. It is going to take nothing less than a mighty surge of the Spirit to get the church going. If we have any hope of evangelizing our world in our generation, we must have revival.

Finally, God gave birth to modern evangelicalism in the heat of a great awakening. Western evangelical Christianity was hewn from the rock of revival. This historical fact is important; we are always to some extent dependent on our past. Over three hundred years ago the Holy Spirit broke into the course of Western Christianity and gave us the great Puritan-Pietist Awakening. In this revival atmosphere most of us have hacked out our understanding of the Christian faith whether we realize it or not. This is why there is always something of a heart cry for revival in the sincere souls of Evangelicals.

The Puritan-Pietist Awakening

Puritanism? Pietism? Today? I realize when I talk about Puritanism and Pietism I am running the risk of running aground. Those words are not too well received in most circles. History has been quite critical of the movement. Even Evangelicals have given these terms their knocks, let alone what those of more liberal persuasions have said. Martin Marty critically states that Pietism was a major stride of Christian retreat from responsibility. Karl Barth spoke of "the inferno of pietism in which the demons do their work." Gibson Winter, secularization theologian at the University of Chicago Divinity School, wrote, "Traditional piety becomes a means of subverting the Gospel and its responsibilities, turning men and women away from their calling to mission." [1] Yet, in a chapel address at Southern Seminary, my colleague Dale Moody honestly confessed, "I'm a Pietist." To clarify his remark, Moody correctly pointed out that the Pietists were not off-putting "Holy Joes," as the term implies to some; the true Pietists simply believed in spiritual, experiential religion. Therefore, I have no reservation in standing with my colleague and stating that, "I'm a Pietist too," and adding, "I'm also a Puritan." For no more than were the Pietists "Holy Joes," the Puritans in their finest expression were not "mean, legalistic, killjoys"; they simply believed in a disciplined, holy life-style.

Moreover, all of us who view our religious faith in the general framework of Evangelicalism have something of the same confession to make. For as I have tried to make clear, mature Puritanism and mainstream Pietism is the rock from

which most modern evangelical Christianity has been sculp-
tured. Yet history has obviously not been very kind, or fair,
to the movement.

One purpose of this chapter is to validate these rather
categorical statements concerning Puritan pietistic influence
and character. Perhaps my implied grievance with history
can be somewhat redressed. Furthermore, we need to understand our roots to make sense of our contemporary ministry. But most important, I want to point out what we today
have lost, or at least forgotten, since the earlier days of the
Great Awakening. In coming to understand what a tremendous thing God did in that significant Puritan-pietistic revival, perhaps we can recapture some of the salient, relevant
features of the movement and thus develop an awareness
of the kind of awakening we need today.

The English Puritan movement and the Continental
Pietist movement should be grasped in the singular. Many
modern historians contend this seventeenth-eighteenth century movement is separated only by the geography of the
English Channel and the temperament and politics of two
different peoples. It is essentially one great move of the
Holy Spirit. For example, Ernest Stoeffler of Temple University states emphatically in his book *The Rise of Evangelical
Pietism,* "the fact is that essential differences between Pietism and what we have called Pietistic Puritanism cannot
be established because they are nonexistent. The pressure
toward a certain pattern of piety within the Calvinistic tradition (regarded broadly) whether in England, the Low Countries, the Rhineland, or elsewhere was basically the same." [2]
Donald Bloesch, a competent authority on the subject, takes
a similar stance, including Quakerism and similar approaches
in the larger movement. [3]

Of course the question can be raised, Why dredge up
an issue such as Puritan-Pietism? Hasn't it been duly con-
signed to the deep by many modern, able thinkers? But it
must be emphasized again, especially for those of us who

long for an awakening, as Stoeffler put it, "the importance of the rise of Pietism for the Protestant experience in general has only recently begun to dawn upon us." [4] I think it *most* important in respect to the kind of revival we need. What, therefore, was this movement trying to say to the church?

The Essence of the Puritan-Pietist Movement

Two things must be made clear before attempting to define Puritan-Pietism. First, only the broad categories of the movement can be considered in this limited space. Fringe aspects such as radical Pietism must be reserved for another time. Therefore, I confess I shall be a bit guilty of generalization but not to a fault I trust. Secondly, to appreciate what these revivalists were saying, they must be seen in historical perspective.

The movement began as the church found itself in the grip of an inordinate quest for theological orthodoxy. As a consequence, the Reformation churches of Europe lost contact with the concerns of daily life. Concentrating their efforts on answering questions no longer being asked and solving problems people did not have, the church simply lost touch with the workaday world. Under these circumstances, "large numbers of nominal Protestants treated their churches with benign neglect, respectfully accepting them as institutions to which one turns to be baptized, married and buried, but which should not be expected to enter vitally into life's concerns." [5] A contemporary quip points out that all the European state church often does for people is to "hatch, match, and dispatch" them. The ivory-tower mentality had shut them in and isolated them from the real world.

Like a descending fog, an irrelevance settled on the established churches in Europe which soon developed into what has been termed a "Protestant Scholasticism." It differed from the syndrome of the Roman Church of the Dark Ages in theology only. The spirit and end product were the same, being a Christian consisted in being correct in doctrine. If you simply believed the right things, you were in. Experience and dynamic force in daily religious life were all but laid to rest. Consequently, "spiritual and ethical sterility" [6] gripped much of the Reformation church.

What a tragedy! And it happened almost immediately after the great reformers, Calvin, Luther, Zwingli, and others, had done their work. It is almost unbelievable how spiritually cold the Reformation churches became in so short a time.

Then just when it seemed that a new "dark age" was about to descend on Europe, the Renaissance notwithstanding, there flashed on the scene a spiritual bolt of lightning. Thousands were suddenly brought into the light of God's presence. Lutherans, Calvinists, Zwinglians, Anglicans, Baptists, and Arminians cried, "Lord Jesus, I want to know you truly and *personally.*" The movement was born! What was the nature of the answer to this pious cry that went up all over the Western world?

The Central Thrust of the Movement

The prime point of the movement is projected in the German word *herzenreligion:* religion of the heart. Here the *heart* refers to the very center or core of personhood. The essential emphasis became total personal involvement in the faith. For the Pietists, faith became inward, experiential, and all-consuming. Although there was heavy weight laid on the objective Scriptures as the source of faith; creeds, mere intellectual assent, and theology were not seen as the essence of real Christianity. For the Pietists faith was not simply outward; it had to affect one's entire being. William Ames, one of the first systematic theologians of Reformed Pietism, stated, "Faith is the resting of the Heart of God." Another significant pietistic thinker held that "in the heart . . . we may know God and the things of God." [7] Jonathan Edwards, who must be included in this train, clearly distinguished between what he termed a "speculative" and a "saving" faith. The former centers around an "assent of the understanding," but saving faith demands "the consent of the heart." [8] He said, "True religion consists so much in the affections that there can be no true religion without them." [9] This must not be seen as anti-intellectualism. Anything but! They never believed a lazy mind honored God. Yet from this basic understanding of faith, as a reaction to the cold orthodoxy of the hour, the movement grew and spread. Several key ideas flowed out of this essential source.

The New Birth

A prominent point of the Puritan-Pietists, as might be expected, was the new birth. While the Reformers, especially Luther, placed emphasis on legal justification, the new voice spoke of the need of regeneration and sanctification. Notable Pietists invariably preached that every person must experience Christ for himself. The experiential element was central. It is surely significant that we have seen a new interest just recently in what it means to be born again, both in books and in personal testimony.

Religious Enthusiasm

Despite all their concern for a religion of the heart, the Pietists were generally distrustful of all forms of religious emotional excesses: raptures, visions, and special revelations. Mainstream Pietism always "tested the spirits" by the objective Scriptures. They contended that following Christ is not emotional so much as it is to bear the fruits of love and obedience to God. Francke, a great Pietist preacher, said, "Love is constant and unchanging, and is to be discovered by your obedience to God, and your patience under trials, rather than by your feelings." [10] Jonathan Edwards confessed, "I had rather enjoy the sweet influence of the Spirit showing Christ's spiritual divine beauty, infinite grace and dying love, drawing forth the holy exercises of faith, divine love, sweet compliance, and humble joy in God one quarter of an hour, than to have prophetical visions and revelations the whole year." [11] Bishop Ryle, the Anglican Puritan warned, "I know no state of soul more dangerous than to imagine we are born again and sanctified by the Holy Spirit, because we have picked up a few religious feelings." [12]

Felicity

Pietism's downplay of excessive emotions is not to imply that this tradition was cold and bereft of feeling. Felicity, joyous feelings of fellowship with Christ in religious experience, was strongly emphasized. To many of the Pietists, dynamic fellowship with Christ that spawns great joy is the goal of all Christian endeavor. To live in intimate, daily fellowship with Christ is the purpose of all creation. The sincere man of faith experiences a sweet foretaste of it in this life and will know its glorious fullness in eternity. The early Dutch Pietist Teellinck prayed, "Lord Jesus, thou dearest groom of my soul . . . when shall I be given the full privilege, to enjoy freely, and with my whole heart, how sweet thou art, my Lord and God. When shall I entirely unite myself with thee?" [13]

Such language surely sounds joyous, actually quite mystical. Are the Pietists mystics? Hans Küng is on target in his work *Freedom Today* when he draws a sharp line of distinction between evangelical faith and medieval mysticism. But many devotional writers of pietistic persuasion have attempted to capture the positive, biblical aspects of mysticism and then synthesize them with traditional, scriptural orthodoxy. For example, George Fox, Richard Baxter, Jeremy Taylor, and others, along with a host of modern Pietists like Andrew Murray, Hannah W. Smith, and Watchman Nee have done good work here. Such an endeavor seems very important to me; felicity is vital to dynamic Christianity.

This leads into the Puritan-pietistic view of sanctification.

Sanctification

Sanctification has always been stressed in this tradition; yet mainline Pietism has constantly attempted to skirt what they considered a heresy, perfectionism. They rarely lost sight of man's sinfulness and the constant need of God's forgiving grace. Francke wrote, "We are not and never will be entirely perfect." [14] Still, Pietism's productiveness in devotional literature is indicative of its constant preoccupation with the spiritual aspects of the Christian life. Their religious idealism was of the highest order. If Puritan-Pietism had any weakness, it was being too concerned with ethical matters. At times they became downright legalistic, but this is to be understood in historical context. Stoeffler reminds us that, "Not to be forgotten is the profound ethical sensitivity of Pietism, a sensitivity which in the Reformed tradition of the seventeenth century was hidden under the bushel of dogmatics." [15] Moreover, this ethical concern was based on their understanding of New Testament morality. Thus it is difficult to fault them too severely. And our permissive society could stand a shot of mature purity and piety.

Biblicism

The New Testament was of vital importance. Because of its biblicism, the movement never degenerated into religious humanism or mere mysticism. Pietists insisted on the absolute authority of the Word of God. Further, they held that the Holy Spirit is able to communicate the truth of the Scriptures to all sincere souls without the necessity of biblical professionals. The Puritan-pietistic tradition would trust the opinions of theologically untrained but dedicated laymen. This was tremendously important in rescuing the doctrine of the priesthood of believers from being no more than a reformed dogma. This approach finally moved the Pietists to the formation of conventicles, private meetings in homes, and Bible study groups where the Scriptures were studied in-depth.

It should be made clear that pietistic biblicism was not legalistic. The spirit, not the letter of the Word, was the constant pietistic quest. For Spener, a great German Pietist, the authority of the Bible was a spiritual one. He held that the scriptural word is dead apart from the testimony of the Holy Spirit. This too is a very important truth.

Pietistic Principles of Christian Education

The intellectual competence of mainstream Pietism was outstanding. They were not mere religious, emotional enthusiasts. That the Pietists were deeply concerned about well-trained Christians is very clear. A cursory survey of the wealth of classical Puritan-pietistic literature is testimony to their intellectual abilities. Writers like William Law, Jeremy Taylor, John Milton, Daniel Defoe, Hermann Francke, John Wesley, Jonathan Edwards, and innumerable others—not to mention classic poets like Isaac Watts and Charles Wesley—should forever dispell any doubt concerning the depth of Puritan-pietistic learning.

Concern for learning was not limited to the clergy alone. There was a deep commitment to an enlightened laity. The principle of small group, in-depth study that was so central to the Pietists is just now being rediscovered by the renewal movement.

What basic philosophy guided this significant stress on Christian education? It had a two-pronged thrust. One, the mind should be trained and filled with a clear analytical grasp of the biblical faith. Secondly, and of equal importance, the heart must be nurtured into a mature, dynamic fellowship with Jesus Christ. Pietists scrupulously attempted to avoid the pitfall of training one in the faith only to see him lose his personal faith in the process. They were utterly convinced a full head without a deep spirit was a travesty for a Christian minister or layman. According to Spener, "the pulpit is not the place for an ostentatious display of one's skills. It is rather the place to preach the Word of the Lord plainly but powerfully." [16] James Stewart, our contemporary, put it this way, "It is difficult for people to see the Lord Jesus through our cleverness."

This approach to Christian education is vital, it seems to me. It may well be this emphasis that kept concern for missionary evangelism at the heart of the Puritan-pietistic Movement.

Missionary Evangelism

Many feel that much of our modern missionary thrust really began with Pietism. The Reformers, as is common knowledge, did not stress world missions and evangelism to the extent many would have wished. It took Pietists like Zinzendorf, the father of the Moravian revival, to say, "My joy until I die . . . (is) to win souls for the Lamb." [17] If Pietism was anything, it was a deep and profound spiritual awakening of worldwide missionary evangelism. All the way from Zinzendorf and the great Moravian movement through the contemporary revivalism of Billy Graham one thing is central: The heart cry of the movement has always been, as expressed by John Knox, "Give me Scotland or I die." In the light of biblical truth, it is difficult to disagree with this Puritan-pietistic insistence on the centrality of worldwide missionary evangelism. In the final analysis this is what Christian ministry is all about. The pietistic awakening had it right.

Social Concern

But can that very attitude be the movement's greatest weakness? Doesn't this insistence on the centrality of evangelism nullify other legitimate concerns, such as man's social needs? History has often accused the Pietists of that perversion. But here again is a case where some historians, past and contemporary, have been unfair to the movement and rendered us all a disservice.

First of all, pietistic evangelism, though individualistic,

was far from superficial. Theologically and practically, strong stress was laid upon in-depth discipleship. Shallow decision making was soundly condemned. Further, extensive instruction for the inquirer after salvation was central.

Secondly, social dimensions in ministry were far from neglected. Francke, for instance, insisted that a concern for meeting social needs is the indispensable fruit of conversion. Spener held a believer should "prove in such service their obedience to God and their love to their fellowmen." [18] As an example of his concern, he influenced the founding of workhouses in Frankfurt, Nuremberg, Augsburg, Leipzig, Halle, and Berlin, as well as schooling for orphans. Francke was instrumental in the establishment of a home for unmarried women, an orphanage, a home for itinerant beggars, a hospital and dispensary, a widows' house, and a home for needy students. He also organized services to the blind, the deaf and dumb, the mentally ill, and on and on. It was out of German and Swiss Reformed Pietism that a whole host of new social movements germinated, grew, and flowered.

Further, the Pietists, and especially the Puritans, were overtly political in that they sought to bring direct pressure on the state to safeguard public morality. Yoder, a noted Mennonite scholar, observed:

It is certainly not the case that pietism whether we think now of the eighteenth century movement or of its more recent spiritual heirs, was uninterested in social or political ethics. Few movements in church history . . . have been . . . so productive of institutional inventiveness and cultural creativity as have been the Moravians, the Methodists, and their counterparts within the larger church.[19]

Well-known is the fact that William Wilberforce, a product of the English revival of the eighteenth century, kept slavery out of Britain. John Wesley, strong for abolition, also instituted medical clinics and even financial credit unions. DeGrellit, a Quaker, was instrumental in prison reform in several European countries. John Woolman was chiefly responsible for the eradication of slavery in Quaker communities in America. Though chided by some for not going further, Charles G. Finney, the American pietistic revivalist, was seriously involved in the American abolition movement. Oberlin College in Ohio where Finney served as professor of theology and president was accused by the Old School Presbyterians of being a "hotbed of revivalism, fanaticism, and social reform."

Time fails to tell of the social work of men like C. H. Spurgeon, William Booth, Robert Raikes, and a multitude of others. Even the modern labor party of Britain grew out of evangelical concern. Hans Küng goes so far as to hold that the perverted New England witch-hunting came to an end in eighteenth-century America in no small part through the influence of mature Pietism. It is quite significant that when Dostoevski in his classic novel *The Brothers Karamazov* wished to describe his beloved character Dr. Herzenstube as a "kind-hearted and human man, who treated the poor and peasants for nothing was held in much esteem and respected by everyone," he called him a Moravian brother. Nineteenth-century people knew the Pietists "had it together," that is, evangelism and social concern. The tradition well understood, as one writer has put it, "a hungry man has no ears." To say that the Puritan-Pietists were mere evangelistic scalp-hunters with little social concern is a gross perversion of historical fact.

Much more should probably be said concerning this vastly diverse movement. For example, they stressed the assurance of salvation, they were pessimistic concerning human rationalism's adequacy to fathom the truth of God, they held a high view of the church, and they had a revolutionary evangelistic spirit. Space forbids these excursions. Perhaps the Puritan-pietistic awakening can be best summarized by simply saying that for the Puritan-Pietist, the good life is to encounter Christ personally, meet the needs of the world, and glorify God.

This leads into a brief historical sweep of the general

awakening that came in the context of the Puritan-pietistic impact. It will help us to understand not only where and when our present-day Evangelicalism was spawned but also will point up the primary principles in the kind of awakening we presently need. A most fascinating circular historical development can be traced.

English Early Beginnings

It is rather difficult to pinpoint the prime patriarch of Puritan-Pietism. The spiritual roots go deep into medieval mysticism. Nonetheless, most historians start with the sixteenth-century preacher, William Perkins of Warwickshire, England. He is considered by many as the progenitor of the pious. A few others claim John Hooper of Somerset was the "morning star" of the movement.[20] Regardless of whom we tap as the beginner, most agree that the movement had its birth in English Puritanism. But even when we say that, it must be admitted that almost simultaneously the new spirit dawned on the Continent. Perhaps the awakening simply burst as the morning sunrise on the whole Western European religious scene among Teutonic peoples. Yet something of a chain of influence can be demonstrated beginning in England.

The theological roots of the thrust are found in the Zwingli-Bucer-Calvin axis of the Reformation. It began to show its early, essential characteristics within English Puritanism and the Dutch Reformed churches of the seventeenth century. These in turn influenced Lutheranism through spiritual giants like Arndt, Spener, Francke, Bengel and their followers. It will help our understanding to see this historical development in more detail.

Many Anglo-Saxons have been fond of linking the phenomenon of Puritanism primarily, if not exclusively, to older, purely English traditions. Yet it seems significant that when the early Puritans quoted books of devotion, they often referred to Continental mystics. Furthermore, in the openness of Edward VI of England to the Continental Reformation, many exiles from the Netherlands, Germany, and even Italy came to London. When they were later forced to leave, along with many Englishmen, under the persecution of Mary, they traveled to Continental centers such as Geneva, Zurich, Basel, Strasbourg, and Frankfurt. In this setting the British-Continental pietistic mix apparently began and the piety of the Reformed tradition sunk its taproot into European soil generally.

Further, Calvin's *Institutes* were translated into English and profoundly influenced early thought. In this Calvinistic context William Perkins made his significant impact. Although he died young, his accomplishments were amazing. He is little known today, yet throughout the seventeenth century his influence in England and the American colonies was regarded as but a little lower than that of Calvin himself. After his untimely death a contemporary wrote, "The precious name of Mr. Perkins shall like an ointment poured forth, fill all quarters of this land with a fresh and fragrant sweetness." [21] Other names linked to the Perkins' tradition were Richard Rogers, John Dod, Henry Smith, and John Cotton of New England.

By the dawn of the eighteenth century, there was what has been called "a flood tide of Godliness." [22] Skyrocketing on the scene came men like John Downame, Daniel Dyke, and John Smith. Stellar spiritual stars were Richard Baxter, the epitome of Puritan-Pietism, John Bunyan of the mighty pen; Jeremy Taylor; and a host of others. By the end of this dramatic century, Puritan-Pietism had the corner on dynamic Christianity in England.

The Move to the Netherlands

Across the English Channel, the churches of pietistic persuasion were unified in spirit under the theological orbit of the Netherlands. Dutch Reformed Pietism was almost the direct result of British Puritan influence. William W.

Teellinck of the Netherlands, who is usually regarded as the father of Continental Pietism, was in England several times and came under the influence of John Dod and Arthur Hilderson. He was actually converted in a Puritan home in Britain. Ames, the early systematic theologian of Dutch Pietism and a most influential leader, was a student at Cambridge and a devoted disciple of William Perkins. At the same time, however, it must be recognized that long standing traditions of piety were native to the Netherlands as personified in men like Gerhard Groote, Ruysbrocek, the Brethren of the Common Life, the Anabaptists, and pre-Reformation mystics such as Coornhert. Yet Teellinck and Ames were deeply indebted to English Puritanism.

A short time later Lodensteyn of Delft arose on the horizon. He was an especially effective preacher and pastor. He shared the convictions of his predecessors, the Puritans and Teellinck. Others followed such as Brakel, John Teellinck (William's son), Saldenus, and deLabadie, the radical Pietist.

At this junction Pietism moved from its early base in the Low Countries and permeated northwestern Germany. The outstanding personality among the early Pietists in Germany was Theodore Untereyck of Mulheim. Studying at Utrecht in the Netherlands, influenced by Lodensteyn and other Dutchmen, he was converted in that pietistic context. Others soon came along, such as Neander the hymnologist, Alardin, and Buchfelder. The German historian Paulus Scharpff tells us that, "because of lively communications between the Reformed of the Netherlands and those of western Germany, Dutch Reformed Pietism was the first of several pietistic movements to penetrate Germany." [23] This surging new movement quickly led to another pietistic movement.

Advent of Lutheran Pietism

The rapid rise of Lutheran Pietism must be viewed against the backdrop of deep-seated religious hostilities, the

Thirty Years War in particular. These socioreligious upheavals molded the German mind for the advent of the awakening. The growing reaction against sterile Lutheranism set the stage along with the foundation already laid in the mystical elements of Luther's own writings. Luther's indebtedness to the mystical writings of Tauler and the Friends of God is clear.

From English Puritanism, through the Dutch, and then into northwest Germany, the movement spread far and wide in Lutheranism. The most significant early personality of Lutheran Pietism was John Arndt (1555–1621). Although he always considered himself a true Lutheran, his pietistic orientation was central in his understanding of Christian experience. Sadly, some of Arndt's followers became extremists. But the influence of John Arndt himself was most significant and widespread, especially through his great work, *True Christianity*. Few devout Lutheran homes would have been without a copy.

Philipp Spener

Others followed in the pietistic historical train until Philipp Jakob Spener (1635–1705) arrived on the scene. Spener grew up in surroundings in which a "mixture of Arndtian and Puritan piety set the tone for daily living." [24] Often called the "name most intimately associated with Pietism," [25] Spener took his master's and doctor's degrees at the University of Strasbourg where he lectured until 1659. Often hearing the preaching of deLabodie, he remarkably combined Arndt's mysticism and practical Puritan attention to daily piety. He rose high in the Christian circles of his day. In 1670 he founded the famous *collegia pietatis* in Frankfurt. This was Spener's term for small Bible study groups. Five years later he published his classical *Pious Desires*. Though a constant center of controversy, he never permitted himself to lapse to the level of his critics. His genuine piety was admired by most. The strain of the controversy, however, finally led to his acceptance of the pastorate of Saint Nicolas in Berlin where he lived out his last years.

Spener's promotion of the *collegia pietatis* was one of the prime factors that sparked the flames of controversy that raged around him. Granted, the idea of small groups meeting to study and deepen the spiritual life of believers—which was the essence of the *collegia pietatis*—was not revolutionary in itself. What fanned the flames was that he offered a definite program to implement the scheme and proceeded to promote it. He felt that the Lutheran Reformation had stopped short at the reformation of doctrine and had failed to include the reformation of life. This approach, as could be expected, was seen as a threat by the traditional establishment. Yet Spener argued that even Luther recognized the principle. Spener thus determined to carry reformed theology to its logical and practical conclusion. This spawned the *collegia* and laid out the program for developing what he called the *eccelesialae in ecclesia*, the true church within the church. His genius is seen in that he was one of the first to grasp the full implications of the priesthood of all believers.

Spener was centrally significant in the entire pietistic movement. He brought the end of one era and ushered in another. Actually, the term *Pietist* was first used in 1664 to designate his Frankfurt disciples. He was a man for the hour—and all seasons. The speculations of the "Protestant schoolmen" no longer attracted the minds of young churchmen. Spener's widespread influence was a severe blow to sterile orthodoxy and brought about a new fresh wind of the Spirit throughout Lutheranism. In a very short time, however, the mantle of Pietism's Elijah was to fall on a young Elisha, August Hermann Francke. Through the ministry of this young prophet, the Lord God of Elijah significantly manifested himself.

A. Hermann Francke

Francke (1663–1727) was born twenty-eight years after Philipp Spener. As Spener was the preaching giant of German Pietism, Francke became its educator par excellence. Trained in the universities of Erfurt, Kiel, and Leipzig, he was destined to become the new central figure of the movement among Lutherans.

After Francke completed his education, he moved to Erfurt to serve as an assistant pastor in a local church. There he began his teaching ministry by presenting practical lectures on the Scriptures for university students. The traditional professors took a dim view of such teaching. Soon he followed his mentor's footsteps in persecution. Pressure mounted until he was actually given only forty-eight hours to get out of town. The very day he received his eviction notice, however, he was appointed professor of Greek and Oriental languages at the University of Halle. In a few years he was elevated to full professor of theology. This fortunate move to Halle came through the influence of his pietistic father, Philipp Spener.

Francke found his life's work at Halle. He was extremely popular with the students, combining intellectual ability with a warm, devoted Christian experience. Through his educational ministry the University of Halle became the radiating center of pietistic influence.

Francke was also an ardent social worker. His creative genius produced a myriad of social ministry, as previously pointed out. He labored in deprived sections of his city and transformed whole areas.

Francke's writings, however, are probably his most significant contribution. His famous *Directions for Profitable Bible Study* was widely read. His works were known and appreciated in all of Europe and America. Susannah Wesley, John Wesley's mother, was a faithful reader. He carried on a voluminous correspondence. The American Puritan preacher Cotton Mather was a constant recipient of his letters. Pietism took the offensive under Francke. Prior to the eighteenth century few attempts at world evangelization were launched, except in a colonialism context. But now a "resurgence of the unquenchable evangelistic spirit in Christianity" [26] was born. In 1705, a small contingency of Halle and Dutch Pietists set out for India. This became the prime move for Protestant mission work in the Far East.

Francke's full contribution to Pietism is difficult to assess. To say the least, he was certainly a turning point in the movement. His social, educational, and missionary emphasis brought profound depth and thrust to the awakening.

The Moravian Revival

Francke's star pupil who was destined for fame and notoriety was Count Nikolaus Ludwig von Zinzendorf (1700–1760). Growing up in a pietistic family (his father was close to Spener), he spent several years studying at Halle. During those days he took his noon meal with Francke himself. The influence of Francke and Halle was most significant on the young count.

After Halle, Zinzendorf studied law at Wittenburg. Yet he could not be content with a career in law. In his own words, his only passion was "to live for the One who had given His life for him, and to lead others to Jesus." [27] In 1727, he was ordained a Lutheran minister.

By 1722, displaced, persecuted Moravian Brethren had begun to gather at Herrnhut, the small village on Count Zinzendorf's estate. In a Herrnhut religious service one Lord's Day, the heavens opened and the great Moravian revival broke. From this outpouring of the Spirit, the whole pietistic movement spread to many distant points.

The history of Moravian missions is legendary. No doubt, Zinzendorf was the guiding spirit and inspiration of the world thrust. He traveled far and near preaching the Word. He sailed to America and was met with much success despite considerable opposition. Five productive years were spent ministering in England. His missionaries touched innumerable places and lives. Scharpff goes so far as to say, "Zinzendorf was undoubtedly the most unique and outstanding personality of eighteenth century pietism in Germany." [28] His contribution was tremendous.

It was through the Moravian contribution that Pietism began to complete its circle of development and move back to Britain where it had begun under the influence of early Puritans like William Perkins.

Back to England and the Eighteenth-Century Awakening

The role played by the Moravians in the Wesleyan drama is well known. Yet the Wesley brothers' conversion was not *wholly* dependent upon Moravian influence, as some would have us believe. For example, various religious societies had emerged in England in reaction to seventeenth-century rationalism. Anthony Harnech of the deLabodie pietistic school significantly influenced those societies, and sensitive minds like the members of Wesley's Oxford Holy Club were deeply impressed. Moreover, Samuel and Susannah Wesley were enthusiastic supporters of these societies. Francke's writings, as we have seen, also influenced the parents of John and Charles. It is also clear that the Wesleys were strongly impressed by the Puritan tradition. This and Whitefield's Calvinism account for the Wesleyan concern for methodical holiness.

Still, it was the Moravian testimony that directly precipitated John Wesley's famous "Aldersgate" experience. John was first made open to this testimony after he saw the calmness of the Moravian Brethren on the storm-tossed ship bound for Georgia on Wesley's voyage to America. This story is often repeated. Later in America, the following interview took place between John and the Moravian bishop, Professor Spangenberg of Jena:

Spangenberg: "Do you know Jesus Christ?"
Wesley: "I know he is the Savior of the World."
Spangenberg: "True, but do you know that he has saved you?"
Wesley: "I hope he has died to save me."
Spangenberg (later): "I fear they were vain words."

After Wesley's so-called failure in Georgia, he returned to England only to confess, "I went to America to convert the heathen, but, oh, who will convert me?" Back in London, Peter Bohler, another Moravian, crossed the Wesley brothers' path. He helped the struggling pair tremendously. Charles soon found a confident faith in Christ and three days later John recorded in his journal:

"Wednesday, May 24, 1738. In the evening I went very unwillingly to the Society in Aldersgate Street, where one was reading Luther's preface to the Epistle to the Romans. About a quarter before nine, while he was describing the change wrought by God in the heart through faith in Christ, I felt my heart strangely warmed. I felt I did trust Christ, Christ alone, for salvation and an assurance was given me that He had taken away my sins, even mine, and saved me from the law of sin and death."

A few months later, along with some Moravian Brethren, the great Fetter's Lane "Little Pentecost" occurred and the revival fully dawned.

George Whitefield had his evangelical experience some two years before the Wesleys had theirs and was preaching very effectively. But now George, John, and Charles joined hearts and arms as never before, and the movement was launched that historians contend saved England from a fate similar to the devastating French Revolution.

Thus with the pietistic writings and the influence of the Moravian movement upon Britain through the Wesley-Whitefield Awakening, mainstream Pietism returned to its English source. This does not mean Puritanism had died in Britain during the development of Continental Pietism. And, of course, important spin-offs impacted various places around the world. But the somewhat circular historical development of the movement from Perkins to the Low Countries, to northwest Germany, into the Lutheran stream, and then from the Moravians back to Britain is quite fascinating. What the English people sowed in germinal Puritanism it bountifully reaped a hundredfold in the great eighteenth-century awakening.

American Foundations

Significant sorties of Puritan-pietistic influence were constantly being sent to the New World during the years of this circular historical development. They took various forms. The writings of the tradition, for example, proved most influential in the colonies. The basic theology of the movement was deeply embedded in New England by the Pilgrim Fathers and in the Middle Colonies by the founding Dutch. Both traditions "were deeply indebted to the earliest Dutch Pietists," especially to the writings of Teellinck and his disciple Voetius. Harvard University's guidebook for young students was penned by Voetius. Further, English Puritan writings, such as those of William Perkins and his pupil William Ames, were translated into Dutch and widely read in Middle America. Huguenot Pietism made itself felt also. John Joy, an ardent Huguenot, founded the American Bible Society, and Peter Stuyvesant's wife was the daughter of a Huguenot pastor.

Puritan-pietistic writings especially abounded in New England, as could be expected. Francke was as widely read as Arndt, Spener, Frelinghuysen, Broheil, Perkins, and scores of others. It is no exaggeration to say the New World was deluged with pietistic writings. Contributions were not all from Europe either. Authors arose in America itself. Prominent personalities like Cotton Mather, Jonathan Edwards, Samuel Finley, Peter Miller, and the Tennents were constantly producing materials. Any Christian of the seventeenth-eighteenth-century America who could read, or even hear, was quite knowledgeable of the tradition.

Nor were the Continental sorties of the Pietists limited to the pen; many preachers made the voyage as well. The Dutchman Frelinghuysen had an extensive, influential ministry in the Middle Colonies as did Peter Miller, Michael Schlatter, and Samuel Guilding who had studied at Halle. Guilding ministered for twenty-five years in Roxburg, Pennsylvania.

Zinzendorf made his presence strongly felt during an extended visit. It is rather puzzling to see the sparks he created. Boehm, Finley, and both Tennents wrote tracts opposing Zinzendorf, and Muhlenberg was sent to America by no less than the Halle Pietists to counteract the Zinzendorf movement. But the impact of the count was profound and Moravian churches still exist in America, not to mention the city of Bethlehem, Pennsylvania, founded by the Moravians—even if today the city is more concerned with steel than the Savior.

All know of George Whitefield's extensive American ministry. Historians differ as to the number of Whitefield's visits, but eleven is probably correct. Tens of thousands hung on his words. He was a preaching giant. Space forbids the accounting of other notables like Francis Asbury, sent by John Wesley himself, Coke, Herneck, and many other evangelical leaders.

Nowhere is this new spirit of Puritan-pietistic evangelism and revivalism in America seen more clearly than in the awakenings of the eighteenth century mentioned in chapter 1. It was this kind of mighty movement of the Holy Spirit that precipitated the first and second great awakenings on American soil. A contemporary pietistic historian has summarized it best by saying that after the first one hundred years of the tradition's arrival in America . . .

Pietism's witness . . . (was integrated) into the fabric of American theology. Pietism had established a new pattern of evangelism and a new form of revivalism; it had opened unforeseen and uncontrived avenues of ecumenism and it had created America's odd mixture of personal piety, moralism, and national faith.[29]

Now all of that is to emphasize this: Although many other influences theologically, socially, and pragmatically have come into present-day evangelical life, it seems very clear to me that our contemporary understanding of evangelism, missions, and experiential religion is the direct child of the great Puritan-pietistic awakening. That is the point of this entire historical chain reaction I have attempted to demonstrate. Pietism is the base on which we modern evangelicals stand. We were born in revival.

But that we have lost something from our Puritan-pietistic heritage in recent years is self-evident. This is serious, if not tragic, it seems to me. Therefore my plea is to regain the positive characteristics of this great revival of dynamic Christianity. I am not asking for a harking back to an old, worn-out tradition so as to retreat into a nostalgic, unreal security. I believe there are very positive features to be regained. These features will obviously need to be realized in contemporary categories; the church must always be relevant to current issues to be effective. But with these principles before us, here is what the coming awakening should incorporate.

Evangelism and Social Concern

The problem of the present-day polarization between social concern and individualistic evangelism must be eliminated. As pointed out, the Pietists "had it together" with remarkable balance. Here is a survey of some of the social services of the Surrey Chapel, a nineteenth-century, London, pietistic church.

1. Almshouses for the poor
2. Band of Hope and Temperance Society
3. Benevolent Society, founded 1785, for relieving the sick poor at their own dwellings by Christian visitors from the

church. About eight hundred cases were relieved yearly.
4. The Christian Instruction Society mapped out the neighborhood into districts, which were visited with tracts.
5. The City Mission had its Surrey Chapel auxiliary, and four missionaries, chiefly supported by the congregation, were always at work among the dense population around.
6. Day Schools were five in number, with seven hundred children.
7. The Dorcas Society assisted poor women in domestic difficulties
8. Female Clothing Society encouraged the poor to deposit their savings, by furnishing articles of clothing at half price.
9. The School of Industry partially clothed fifty girls, and instructed them in needlework and housework, as well as in reading.
10. The Sunday School Society embraced thirteen different organizations.
11. The Southwark Mission, for the elevation of the working classes.

Yet at the same time, the gospel was proclaimed and people converted. This is the way church life should be lived out. The New Testament knows no polarization between social service and evangelism. People are social *and* individualistic creatures and hence have both kinds of needs. We should simply step in and meet them all as we have opportunity and resources. Our stance must never be either-or; it must be both-and. Our pietistic forefathers saw this clearly. So must we if we are to minister effectively in today's kind of complex, pluralistic world.

Theology and Feeling

The Puritan-pietistic tradition, in the second place, had a beautiful balance between theology and felicity. For the better part these people were highly educated in the biblical faith. They never countenanced a slothful mind. Yet they were a deep feeling people. Recent history is even reevaluating the so-called somber Puritans. They were not as somber and stoical as some would have us believe. There is joy and peace in the assurance of faith—and they promoted it. Witness the hymns of Isaac Watts, John Fawcett, Charles Wesley, and others. Head and heart are Christ's concern. You can have a head full of truth and a heart full of love and joy in Jesus Christ. This, to me, is a prize to be sought most earnestly.

Christian Education

This implies another facet of current need, namely, a balance in Christian education. That the Pietists were deeply committed to a highly educated ministry and laity is patent. American witness to this fact is Harvard, Rutgers, Brown, Princeton, and other great universities founded by the Puritan-Pietists. Yet they firmly believed a servant of Christ was *not* educated with merely a head crammed with knowledge. He must have a deepening and maturing spiritual life. In pietistic terms, his soul must be cultivated and enlarged as well as his mind. But Wayne Oates is probably correct when he says there is in our theological schools today "a conspiring of silence about personal religion." [30] In defense we comment that our schools and church educational programs cannot be "three-year camp meetings." But I ask, in some senses, *why not?* If we leave our learning experience without a deep, rich, warm, and winsome spiritual experience, are we truly prepared for service? I seriously doubt it. Academics? By all means! But we must combine it with a contagious religious experience. As has been said, "A full heart does not necessarily mean an empty head." It seems we find this principle very difficult to effect. Yet we must strive to inject this balance in our training. Our churches deserve men and women *of God* in the full sense of the word. Here is a page we can take from the pietistic workbook on theological education as we search out the kind of awakening we need. A real revival does not put the brain or heart in neutral.

The Devotional Life

The Puritan-pietistic tradition had a strong emphasis on the disciplined life. Our needs in this respect are obviously paramount. Devotional Bible study, intercessory prayer, thankful adoration of God, the Lord's Day observance, protracted prayer, simplicity, and fasting were all a part of their Christian life-style. George Whitefield said, "Whole days and weeks have I spent prostrate on the ground in silent or vocal prayer." [31] Rather strange words in today's undisciplined Christian life-styles! But perhaps this is the reason we are not seeing what Whitefield saw in his ministry.

The Holy Life

The tradition was vitally concerned about a holy life—and that in a mature, wholesome sense. Stoeffler correctly states that the *central* concern of the Pietists was holiness.[32] They were Puritans; they believed in purity. They were Pietists; they believed in piety. If their temptation was a "holier than thou" attitude, ours today seems to be a "worldlier than thou" spirit. All are tempted but we need not yield. The Puritan-pietistic tradition always strove for a winsome holiness that emanates from the love and joy and peace effected by the indwelling Spirit. Our Lord called for holiness (1 Pet. 1:15). So should we.

Place of the Laity

Moreover, the Pietists appear two hundred years ahead of their time in their emphasis on the importance of the laity in ministry. They took seriously the full implications of the doctrine of the priesthood of all believers. A "prominent role (was) assigned to lay leaders." [33] They also embraced a very responsive attitude toward the leadership of women.[34] It would be incorrect to say they had a seventeenth-century women's lib movement going, but they were certainly ahead of their time—and even ahead of some of us. Their fresh attitude towards lay involvement is perhaps best seen in their small-group activities, for example, the *collegia pietatis* in Germany and the Epworth societies under Wesley in England. Groups were not invented by the contemporary renewal movement. Hundreds of years ago, small groups and lay leadership were used significantly by the tradition.

Missionary Evangelism

Finally, the Pietists' greatest contribution was the injecting of the missionary spirit into the Reformation. Bringing the message of God in Christ to the whole world was their deep concern. Nor can they be accused of precipitating a shallow evangelism. Dietrich Bonhoeffer would have been welcomed with open arms among the early Pietists with his "costly grace" principle.

The depth of commitment to the evangelistic task through the entire history of the pietistic movement is truly inspiring. Time fails to speak of Richard Baxter "preaching as a dying man to dying men," or John Bunyan writing in the Bedford jail, incarcerated because of his fearless preaching of the gospel, or William Carey praying before a world map for the conversion of the nations as he made shoes in his little Northamptonshire shoe shop, or David Brainerd who said: "I cared not where or how I lived, or what hardships I went through, so that I could but gain souls to Christ. While I was asleep I dreamed of these things, and when I awoke the first thing I thought of was this great work. All my desire was for the conversion of the heathen, and all my hope was in God."

These are the world's change agents. Whether it be a scholarly Jonathan Edwards or the simple in faith like Hudson Taylor, this is the spirit that has brought the church to its highest hours. President Franklin D. Roosevelt has told us, "Never has a man of ease left a mark on history." To put it in modern jargon, those who "play it cool" do not change their times.

Conclusion

Therefore, the need seems paramount for a rekindling of these principles and spirit that centers in fervent, in-depth, theologically aware, missionary-evangelistic minis-tries. Our contemporary situation surely calls for another awakening to revive the church such as the Puritan-pietistic tradition conceived. This is the kind of revival we need. A great church leader recently stated, "The First Great Awak-ening has run out" in American church life. It is time to seek another such move of God upon us. When will it come? What will it be like for us today?

6

When the Awakening Comes: Principles of True Revival for Today

February 3, 1970, began much like any other college day for Asbury College and Seminary, nestled in the beautiful bluegrass country of central Kentucky.

Asbury is quite similar to any other small, American Christian college. It did have a few things that somewhat set it apart however. There had been a profound spiritual awakening on the campus in 1950, and the students were praying for another. But that crisp February Tuesday dawned like many that had preceded it.

The student body assembled for their regular chapel hour at 10 A.M. The service opened as usual when suddenly, as one student expressed it:

There came a spontaneous movement of the Holy Spirit. I have never witnessed such a mighty outpouring of God upon His people. The scene is unbelievable. The altar has been flooding with needy souls time and time again. Witness is abundant. Release-Freedom-There are tears. Repentance-Joy unspeakable-Embracing-Spontaneous applause when a soul celebrates. A thousand hearts lifted in songs of praise and adoration to a Mighty God.[1]

An awakening had come!

The Asbury event is one of the great awakenings experienced in recent times in America. It is important for us because from it and similar outpourings of the Holy Spirit we can discover the pietistic revival principles that always seem to occur when God visits his people. To understand these principles is vital for three reasons. First, it can provide an insight to what God may be doing through the previously discussed renewal, charismatic, and deeper-life movements and how they can figure in a general awakening. Secondly, we should be able to see the genuine relevance to our day of the essential features of the historical Puritan-pietistic movement discussed in the previous chapter. Thirdly, we need to be aware of how God works in revivals so that when the awakening we need does come, we can intelligently cooperate with the Holy Spirit as the Puritan-Pietists so ably did. Consequently we will be able to further the work rather than impede it as the undiscerning in the church have so often done.

The Principles of Spiritual Awakenings

In an old classic, *Revivals, Their Laws and Leaders*, James Burns projects several "laws" or principles of great awakenings. The affinity between these so-called laws and the various movements discussed in the previous chapters will become obvious. Burns tells us first that a revival always moves forward and generates new life as it surges in and through the church.

The Law of Progress

God is progressively active in our world. That is axiomatic. This progressive work of God is not a steady, stabilized move upward however. It ebbs and flows; seemingly a protracted period of little movement, then suddenly a fresh surge of the Spirit lifts the church to the heights. Although the general trend of God's work is always upward, the progress is characterized by ups and downs. The ups are the revival times.

How vital these revival seasons are! Burns states,

"Revivals are necessary for the spurring of man to high endeavor, and for the vitalizing of life. Were progress to be uniform— no part of man's nature moves until the other parts move also— advance would be so slow that life would stagnate. There could then be no high hopes, no springtide of exulting life, no eager and impetuous rush forward. Progress would be so slow as to be imperceptible, and man, robbed of high inspiration, would cease to hope, and cease to struggle. By the breath of revival life, however, God keeps the world in eager activity, and keeps the human heart ever fresh with hope." [2] The consequence: progress and growth.

Out of the Asbury awakening unbelievable spiritual progress took place. An eyewitness expressed it this way:

As news of the Asbury revival spread across the country, hundreds of pastors began requesting student teams to come and share the story with the members of their congregations. Every Saturday for the next several months, a large procession of cars left Wilmore, headed for all points of the compass. Many students traveled by air to distant assignments.

Almost invariably, wherever the witness teams went, the results were the same. Pastor and people responded. The sermon and order of service were pushed aside for the moment. Many church members, tired of pretending for so long, took off their masks and exposed their own hypocrisy and phoniness. Broken in spirit, they openly confessed their needs, prayed and shared with one another. Church altars which for years had been nothing more than pieces of furniture now became hallowed places where men met God and brother was reconciled to brother. The usual stiffness and formality gave way to a new freedom in the Spirit. With hearts full of joy, members of the congregation lifted their hands in the air and sang forth the praises of God. [3]

Something like this kind of progress always typifies true awakenings.

The Law of Spiritual Growth

Above all, revivals are God's instrument for revitalizing spiritual life. When awakenings occur, Christians are never quite the same again. Whoever and wherever it touches volcanic change erupts. The Asbury awakening was not extensive in its geographical impact. Where it did reach, however, lives were radically changed. One professor said this of his experience:

We found ourselves walking in a sense of reverent awe, our minds racing with questions, our wills painfully adjusting to the demands of what God had wrought, our hearts reaching out in eager desire to tell others, and our souls lifted in glorious joy, praise, and new dimensions of loving adoration of the Lord.[4]

The movement deepened all. As mentioned, the revived students went everywhere sharing their experience. A friend told me that a group came to his church in Texas. As these eager students simply shared what God had done, the Holy Spirit fell mightily on the church and great blessings flowed. This happened wherever the students went. And though the movement never reached beyond the student body and where they ministered, everything was literally transformed as the Holy Spirit extended the work.

At other times, however, the Spirit engulfs large, extensive areas. The great fifteenth-century Florentine revival under Savonarola remade Florence, Italy, into a veritable city of God on earth. The Welsh revival of 1902–1904 so radically altered the entire Rhondda Valley of Wales that the animals employed to bring up coal from the mines had to be taken out of the collieries and retrained. Prior to the awakening, they responded only to cursing. So many miners were converted that with their language cleaned up the colliery animals did not know how to work. The whole Church of Wales came alive as never before. For months many churches stayed open twenty-four hours a day. Tens of thousands were converted.

Revival results are always the same: profound spiritual growth. This is true whether limited or extensive in geographical impact. For, "the law which moves the mighty tides of the ocean is the same which ruffles the surface of the little pool made by the rain of a summer afternoon."[5]

The Law of Periodicity

Law implies an orderly sequence of movements. Do revivals exhibit this kind of movement? Do awakenings occur at definite intervals? Can these sequences be discerned? If that were possible, we could forecast their appearance with some precision. But this is obviously not the case.

History is full of instances where churches have felt a desperate need for revival only to experience little blessing. Then when least expected, the heavens opened. Clearly, the term *law* in this context must not be interpreted legalistically. The Spirit moves as he wills. Yet we may believe that these periodic movements operate on what we call "Divine law," on the basis of the inscrutable hidden purposes of God.

This law of periodicity reveals several important facts. First, God is in control of his church and will give his people what they need when they need it. Secondly, God's wisdom far supersedes ours, and we must always place the timing of these awakenings in the divine economy of things. Thirdly, revivals do not come by caprice or just because the church does certain things in a formal, structured fashion. Although the people of God have their part—a part we will discuss in detail later—the sovereignty of God is central. The law is not mechanical. Perhaps it is best summarized by saying the needs and activity of the church and the sovereignty of God form the warp and woof of genuine revival.

The Ebbing Tide. A general defection from "the faith once delivered to the saints" usually infects the church just before awakenings come. Dullness and lethargy pervade God's people. Dark days settle in. These periods are further characterized by straying from the central task of evangelism. Churches and pastors begin to substitute secondary ministries for this primary responsibility. Priorities get reversed.

Along with these problems, deviations from apostolic theology subtly creep in, and the absolute authority of the Bible begins to be questioned. Compromise on ethical and moral principles tends to follow hard on the heels of doctrinal errors. A critical and blasé attitude envelops many as people grow cynical about those whom they label as "puritanical" and "pious." Not a few actually defect and fall into open sin. In a word, plain old worldliness takes over, and the church sinks into a Laodicean syndrome. Yes, the program goes on, often with greater fervor. But spiritual power is strangely missing, and with the church neither hot nor cold, it stands in dire danger of the Lord's Laodicean rejection (Rev. 3:16).

Although ebb and flow in church vitality seems inevitable, the church and the individuals who make up the church are not thereby exonerated and blameless for their defections. In the final analysis we become what we want to become, and we bear the consequences of our own actions. We reap what we sow, individually and collectively.

Although the depth of depression of one generation may not sink to the depth of previous times (God takes his church constantly higher), the ebbing tide always characterizes the world generally, and especially the people of God, before the awakening comes. For example, Italy and the controlling church was unbelievably corrupt before the great Franciscan revival. The general moral level was very low. The Hebrides awakening of 1949 was preceded by widespread spiritual apathy and general unconcern. And although Asbury College and Seminary was far from apostate, it genuinely needed a fresh touch of God. Application of this law to our contemporary situation is obvious. But more of that later.

The Fullness of Time. The ebbing spiritual tide has its limits as surely as the ebb tide of great oceans. Apathy and coldness has its end. For this we must thank God. Actually, the further the tide ebbs, the greater power and force it gains to return and overflow the arid land.

The ebb tide seems to create among God's true people a deep sense of dissatisfaction. A period of gloom settles in—even to the point of weariness and exhaustion. Sick in soul and heart, men turn to God with a deep sigh. Asbury prayed and prayed. Wales prevailed before God in an agony of spirit. A faithful few prayed night after night into the early morning hours until the Hebrides revival broke.

Where are these burdened believers found? We must recognize that even in the darkest hours, the church always contains those who have not bowed the knee to Baal during the ebb tide. In these precious few the burden and aching grows. Finally, longing for better things becomes intense pain, and the burdened determine with Jacob of old, "I will not let thee go, except thou bless me" (Gen. 32:26). And though God may well touch their thigh and they limp through the rest of their days, *they prevail. Revival is always born in prevailing prayer.* This is the one, basic, unalterable, central principle of awakenings. Prayer opens the door to the fullness of time.

Illustrations of this central significant fact are endless. Dig deep enough in any revival, and you will *always* find a praying group. Let one example among thousands point up this prime principle. On the island of Lewis in 1949 prior to the Hebrides awakening (which was in many respects much like the old Welsh revival), the tide had ebbed far. Few went to church. Little wonder, the churches were apathetic and spiritually inept. Secularism, materialism, and worldliness was the general life-style of the island. Then God laid the burden of prayer on two different small groups.

A few men began praying in a barn outside their village. They prayed two, three, four nights a week into the small hours of the morning. The burden of their agonizing sacrificial prayer was for an awakening. This little group, as one author expressed it, "entered into a covenant with God that they would give Him no rest until He had made Jerusalem a praise in the earth." [6]

At the same time, two old, godly sisters began praying. They also prayed night after night. Impressed by the Holy Spirit, the praying sisters asked their pastor to contact Duncan Campbell in England to lead their church in a preaching mission. The pastor discerned that the request was of God and invited Campbell to Lewis. The evangelist replied that he was completely booked for a year, but if any opening occurred he promised to come. In a matter of days virtually all of his engagements were cancelled. The whole affair clearly being directed by the Holy Spirit, Campbell traveled to the Hebrides and became God's prophet in the awakening. The point of it all is that God *always* lifts up small praying groups when the fullness of time comes.

The application to our need is obvious. If revival comes today, there must be praying people who take their intercession for an awakening with deadly seriousness. But where are they? We seemingly will do anything, make any sacrifice, go anywhere, *except* pray. Oh, where are the prayer warriors of times past? Will God raise up such groups in our day? We must defer the answer to this central question to the last chapter.

The Emergence of the Prophet. Revivals have leaders. Sometime one, sometimes many. These leaders tend to be the incarnation of the movement; they personify the awakening in its most intense form. History is replete with this principle. It starts in the Bible with Shem, goes through giants like Noah, Abraham, Deborah (women are in this galaxy), Samuel, David, the prophets, John, the apostles, and Paul. It continues through historical figures like the church fathers, Francis of Assisi, Bernard of Clairvaux, Savonarola, right up to the Reformation and the Puritan-pietistic revival.

The leader is critically important. He gathers up all those intangible longings and ideas dimly felt and grasped by the masses and then personifies them, epitomizes them, sharpens them, expresses them, and gives them startling visibility. His authority is evident as he gives substance to the many factors of the movement.

Revival leadership is a two-way street; the prophet effects the movement and vice versa. He brings his own individuality to the awakening and to some extent shapes and molds it. At times the leader so epitomized the thrust that a casual look might draw one to the conclusion that the leader was the creator. But he is a product of the movement himself. He can never do what he does unless he, too, is one of the awakened.

The leader is normally called upon to pay a high price. The drain and strain can be tremendous. In John Wesley's journal we read, "March 17, 1752. At the Foundry. How pleasing it would be to flesh and blood to remain at this little quiet place, where at length to weather the storm! Nay, I am not to consult my own ease but the advancing of the kingdom of God." Evan Roberts, the prophet of the Welsh revival, was so shattered by the work that he was never able to preach again. He lived out his days in relative isolation in the home of Jessie Penn-Lewis. Savonarola was burned at the stake. That was his price to pay.

Although every leader, and hence every awakening, is unique and may differ radically in temperament and emphasis, they still possess a common denominator. Burns puts his finger on this when he says,

Each of these great leaders has in common with all the others an unshakable faith in God, an overwhelming sense of a call to great service, a mysterious equipment of spiritual power which moves mountains, and a determination to do the work he is called of God to do even at the expense of life itself. In the Picture Gallery of the good and great, such men occupy the noblest place.[7]

The Law of Variety

Each revival has a uniqueness of its own, as stated. No awakening is identical with any other in particular. As society changes from one generation to the next, as people differ in temperament and culture, so the revival must vary to be relevant to its time and place. There seemingly cannot be a single movement that reaches all peoples and all cultures. For example, the Wesley ministry revolutionized the English but left the Scots cold. The Welsh revival stopped short at the border of England, although it broke out in

Welsh congregations all over the world. Even the Reformation primarily touched the Teutonic people and left the Latins unmoved.

But this is the wisdom of God. If all revivals were cast-iron in their program, large masses would obviously go unreached. The movement must express itself in the cultural context of particular people. This is the only way it can be relevant to real life.

Another striking fact is the vast variety of appeals in awakenings. At times the emotional impact predominates, as in the frontier revival of nineteenth-century America. At other times theological aspects dominate, as in the Reformers. Then again volitional decision making is paramount. This was the Wesleyan thrust. But each movement wins its way because of the particular needs of particular people at particular times.

Further, each movement usually stands in contrast to the previous one. If the watchword of a revival is freedom in Christ, the next may well be the authority of Christ. The extreme of one emphasis usually demands the extreme of the next to effect a general balance. An illustration of this principle is the Oxford movement of the early nineteenth century with its stress on spiritual authority as a conservative reaction to the extremes of the evangelical revival in the Church of England. This phenomenon can also be seen in the new authority system that is beginning to develop in the excesses of the contemporary charismatic revival.

Yet in it all God is at work and effecting a balance. And through the law of variety, the Spirit of God builds up the church.

The Law of Recoil

Every revival ends. It has its day. Luther said that thirty years was the outer limit of an awakening. Though Luther is probably correct concerning most cases, some revivals have lasted considerably longer. Significant awakenings have been burning in Uganda, the Ukraine, and Rumania for years. But all awakenings finally end. The immediate impact of the Asbury revival lasted only a matter of four or five years. Recoil seems inevitable.

The first check of the awakening often comes when the initial emotional tidal wave has run its course. The many who were swept along on the merely emotional level soon fall away. Of course, the more stable effects hang on long after the first emotional excitement dies. The church and society are always left on a higher plane.

The churches in Wales are a classic case of the early demise of an awakening. Not too long ago I was driven up the Rhondda Valley. My host pointed to church after church whose congregation numbered only fifteen to twenty-five members. It was hard to believe that not many decades ago these buildings could not hold the people and never closed their doors for months.

Even when an awakening is long lasting, the long-term effects eventually evaporate and decay sets in. The Franciscan revival is an example. In the midst of a corrupt religious scene, "never since the birth of Christianity has anything appeared on earth more pure or fair than that movement as first conceived by its originator [St. Francis], or practiced by his followers." [8] Yet within a hundred years the vow of poverty had turned to riches, humility to tyranny, monasteries to palaces, and confession into manipulation. The deterioration so eroded the positive influence of the revival it finally turned it sour.

Therefore, when the awakening comes, this law of recoil must be recognized and prayerfully anticipated. This can help minimize the impact of the reality and save many a tragedy.

The Law of Theology

Theology changes during revival times. There always seems to be a return to conservative evangelical thought. It takes this course:

1. A return to simplicity. Believers break through complex, abstract, obscure theology and get to the basic practical truth of the Scriptures. In a word, they become evangelical in thought and theology.

2. A return to New Testament spirit and methods. There is a quest for the apostolic faith and way of doing things. The spirit of the first church is sought. The Bible becomes the pattern for service.

3. The message of the cross. The gospel, the *kerygma*, that centers in the cross of Christ becomes the focal point of preaching. As Charles H. Spurgeon expressed it (his ministry was born in revival), "I take my text and make a beeline to the cross."

4. The salvation of Christ as man's greatest need. In awakenings evangelism thrusts itself to the fore. Secondary ministries—as important as they are—are put in their proper secondary place and winning people to personal faith in Christ becomes central. If people without Christ are lost, as the Bible says, evangelism must come first. A former president of the seminary in which I teach said, "It is such a pity that preachers do not keep to the main thing, the winning of lost souls to Christ." [9] Awakenings restore proper priorities. Redeeming love is the theme.

5. Liberal, rationalistic, speculative theology dies. That kind of thought system never brings about awakenings. This does not mean revivals spawn anti-intellectualism. That too is a perversion of the Spirit's work. This has surely been made crystal clear in the pietistic movement. But an empirical, purely rationalistic, liberal theology that downgrades the transcendental elements of Christianity are laid to rest in awakenings. People are made vividly alive to the fact that this transcendental miracle-working God is among them—and breaking in on the causal continuity of history.

6. Cold orthodoxy is reawakened. Although orthodoxy

is always, I suspect, "my-doxy," we know what we mean by the orthodox faith. And we further know that conservative theological systems can soon cool off and stagnate. Nothing is much "deader" than a dead, cold, rationalistic fundamentalism. But when revival comes, though the actual theological position of conservatives may not substantially change, it suddenly comes alive and glows. That change is as needed as an overhauling of so-called liberal theology.

Conclusion? We need a theological revival as well as a moral, ethical, ministering awakening.

The Law of Consistency

Revivals differ. This is clear. Yet there are certain, consistent elements that always seem to appear. In the coming awakening, I'm sure we will see it expressed in the culture, language, needs, and context of our own particular situation. But I am also sure the following general revival characteristics will be found, although expressed in relevant ways.

First, when the awakening breaks, a deep sense of sin will be awakened. In the intense awareness of God's presence, individual guilt overwhelms the sensitized hearts of the participants, and not just conviction over heinous sins of the flesh alone. Secret and seemingly insignificant sins become a deep burden. When the Asbury revival erupted, the chapel did not close for three days. Those many hours were spent in confession and testimony. It has always begun like that.

I was preaching in a little church in Alabama some time ago. God's Spirit moved deeply. Many began confessing sins in an after-service prayer meeting. I'll never forget one teenager confessing to stealing a saltshaker from a restaurant as a prank. She brokenly prayed for forgiveness and told God if she could remember where she got it, she would take it back. That may seem almost silly, at least rather trite. But stealing is stealing, and it was a real burden to her young sensitive heart. Furthermore, it brought about deep dedication. She later married a minister and is a profoundly spiritual pastor's wife to this day.

Another principle is implied in the above illustration. Restoration, as far as possible, must be made. Jim Vaus, a man involved in syndicated crime before his conversion in Billy Graham's first 1949 crusade in Los Angeles, made restitution for all he had stolen. It wiped him out financially. He even changed his testimony in a court case where his perjury had sent an innocent man to jail. Paul said, "I exercise myself to have a conscience void of offence toward God *and* toward *men"* (Acts 24:16).

The Fullness of the Spirit. Another facet in our revival jewel that always glistens brightly is the fullness of the Holy Spirit. After cleansing comes fullness. The Bible abounds with this idea: "And they were all filled with the Holy Spirit and began to speak in other tongues, as the Spirit gave them utterance" (Acts 2:4). "And when they had prayed, the place in which they were gathered together was shaken; and they were all filled with the Holy Spirit and spoke the word of God with boldness" (Acts 4:31). "And to know the love of Christ, which surpasses knowledge, that you may be filled with all the fullness of God" (Eph. 3:19). "And do not get drunk with wine, for that is debauchery; but be filled with the Spirit" (Eph. 5:18). An objective view of the Scriptures forces the conclusion that God wants his people filled with his Holy Spirit.

God always does this climactic work in an awakening. Christians need such a crisis to bring them to consecration. People need power for service. The faithful need fullness to bear fruit. All need a profound touch of God in their lives. That which the Holy Spirit does in guidance (Rom. 8:14), prayer help (Rom. 8:26), sealing (Eph. 1:13), enlightenment (John 16:13), conviction (John 16:7–11), and exalting

of Christ (John 16:14) must become an experiential reality.
God effects it all by filling his people with the Spirit. An
awakening invariably quickens this experience.

All three renewal movements being considered have
to some extent seen this. Of the three, however, the Keswick
emphasis has grasped the idea most clearly. This is one of
the reasons I see Keswick more in line with the biblical
principle of revival. When one digs into actual awakenings,
Keswick theology and revivals—as is becoming increasingly
evident—have an amazing affinity and similarity.

Regardless of what God uses to revive his work, he always fills his people with the power of the Holy Spirit. And
the Spirit exalts Jesus Christ and infuses vitality into everything he touches. Few would like to refute that blessing.

Fullness of Joy. Thirdly comes the flood tide of joy. After
cleansing and fullness, God pours out his Spirit of love, joy,
and peace (Gal. 5:22). The happiest people who have ever
lived are the revived. Burns states, "There is a joyousness
and elasticity of spirit, and a hopefulness. . . . This is the
effect of a revival wherever it appears. It irradiates the atmosphere; it leaves in its track numberless happy men and
women whose faces are aglow with a new light, and whose
hearts throb with an intense and pure joy." [10]

This explains why the awakened Christian church has
always been a singing people; "Where the Spirit of the Lord
is, there is liberty" (2 Cor. 3:17). So many churches today
are somber and joyless. Little wonder the outsider is not
attracted. I do not speak of shallow "hip hip hooray Christianity." That too is off-putting. I speak of a genuine joy that
blooms out as the fruit of the Spirit. That always attracts.

Effective Evangelism. The effulgence of joy leads to the
fourth characteristic of awakenings, evangelism. Joy must
be shared. The church burns to bring others to Christ, and
the unbelieving community is so attracted by what is going
on in the church that they come by the multitudes to dis-

cover what is happening. It is exactly like the events on the day of Pentecost (Acts 2). When the Spirit falls on the church, the multitudes come and are "bewildered" (v. 6, RSV), "amazed and wondered" (v. 7, RSV), "amazed and perplexed" (v. 12, RSV) and finally throw up their hands in intellectual despair and cry out, "What does this mean?" (v. 12, RSV). This becomes the context of great outreach. When unbelievers begin to ask questions, instead of criticizing, then the gospel can be effectively communicated.

In a word, when God can break in on the church and truly revive his people, then the Spirit can reach the lost in unprecedented numbers. Acts 2 ends with about three thousand converts (v. 41), and even more marvelous, "the Lord added to their number day by day who were being saved" (v. 47, RSV).

Furthermore, those converted in the spirit of awakenings are normally growing, maturing believers. Those who were converted on the Day of Pentecost "devoted themselves to the apostles' teaching and fellowship, to the breaking of bread and the prayers. . . . They sold their possessions and goods and distributed them to all, as any had need. . . . praising God and having favor with all the people" (vv. 42, 45, 47, RSV). This is always the case. Even though the Welsh revival dissipated in a generation, those who were converted in the awakening continued steadfast to the end. I talked once with a dear, old Welsh saint who could remember those revival days. She was as close to Christ in her latter years as in the early days of her spiritual journey.

Lay Involvement. In the fifth place, laymen at long last get geared for ministry. Pastors have challenged, pleaded, even begged the lay folk to give their time and energies in service—probably even to a fault. Still the majority of the laity are merely passive spectators. Thank God for the faithful few, but they are so few. These few will never turn the blitz of Satan as "the few" in the Battle of Britain turned the Nazi tide in World War II. *All* the people of God must get into the warfare. Even the renewal, charismatic, and Keswick movements, despite their great contributions, have failed right there. This point I have stressed. When an awakening arrives, however, the whole company of Christians are so revived that service for Christ abounds everywhere. Every revival is testimony to this principle. Asbury students went nationwide testifying. The Welsh laity became great witnesses. Every revived American frontiersman became an evangelist. Wesleyan lay folk were the great social workers. The illustrations are endless.

I do not believe we will ever see the multitudes of laity motivated, enlisted, equipped, and sent out in ministry until an awakening comes. Does this mean we should stop challenging them? Should we give up the renewal emphasis in our churches? Never! We must continue to call out the few, but the ultimate answer for lay involvement is revival.

Ethical Change. The sixth principle states that great moral and ethical advances are made. In Wales the jails emptied and crime all but ceased. Finney saw entire towns converted and civic righteousness established. As pointed out, the vileness of the American frontier was eradicated and the pioneers sang hymns as they moved westward. All real revivals are ethical and moral revivals. Furthermore, ethics that do not grow out of a theological and spiritual base are at best dignified humanism and erected on the foundations of sand that cannot finally stand the storm.

Revivals Spread. In the final place, when the awakening comes, it will spread like wildfire. It always has. Even on the primitive, slow-moving American frontier, when the awakening broke, the whole area was set ablaze in a matter of months. Now, with our means of mass communication and rapid transportation, it should spread with incredible speed.

In the light of all that has been said, surely our hearts well up with the cry of the psalmist as he prayed:

When the Lord turned again the captivity of Zion, we were like them that dream. Then was our mouth filled with laughter, and our tongue with singing: then said they among the heathen, The Lord hath done great things for them. The Lord hath done great things for us; whereof we are glad. Turn again our captivity, O Lord, as the streams in the south. They that sow in tears shall reap in joy. He that goeth forth and weepeth, bearing precious seed, shall doubtless come again with rejoicing, bringing his sheaves with him (Ps. 126:1–6).

Awakening Signs

Can we honestly anticipate this kind of revival today? I realize I have assumed we can. In attempting to justify my assumption concerning an awakening in our time, let me first share a conviction. I feel that the church of Jesus Christ is certainly not on the verge of extinction; in my considered opinion it is on the edge of awakening. The question is not, *Will* the church be revived? One may just as well ask, "Will the sun rise in the morning?" The issue is, *When* will God's people be revived? I feel God is trying to say to us today what he said to Israel long ago: "Comfort, comfort my people, says your God. Speak tenderly to Jerusalem, and cry to her that her warfare is ended, that her iniquity is pardoned" (Isa. 40:1–2, RSV). The day is at hand.

When will revival come? Burns describes several "straws in the wind." For example, an awakening normally meshes in synchronization with national events. When social, political, and economic crises develop, revival is often God's solution. As we look at the sociological revolution we have endured for the last two decades, the present apathy notwithstanding, all our hearts should resound in an anticipatory cry for revival.

Another "straw" indicating the coming awakening is the feeling of helplessness in the church to cope with all its problems. Thankfully, there are many bright spots and considerable positive thought regarding church growth. Yet many congregations are to some degree in despair, and despair is negative and destructive. But if this despair can deepen into burden, there is real hope. If despair can drive us to prayer, it is positive.

Finally, when there is concern for world missions and evangelism, an awakening may be imminent. It has been many years since there has been such enthusiasm for the evangelization of our world in our generation than there is right now. All these factors must surely mean something in the sovereign plan of God for revival. Could it be that the awakening is on the way?

No one has grasped these principles more clearly than Charles G. Finney. If anyone can understand awakening signs, it is Finney. I see him as one of America's greatest revivalist. He is most helpful because he hammered out his ideas in the white-hot fervor of one of America's profound spiritual awakenings. We will be wise to investigate what he has to say. But obviously, we must grasp his principles from our contemporary, cultural vantage point.

Finney's Principles

Finney first finds the prophet Habakkuk praying the proper prayer: "O Lord, revive thy work in the midst of the years, in the midst of the years make known; in wrath remember mercy" (Hab. 3:2). The preacher anticipated anguish; Judah's defeat and captivity were at hand. So the prophet prayed, "O Lord, revive thy work." It is as if he said, "O Lord, grant that thy judgments may not make Israel desolate. In the midst of these awful years, let the judgments of God be made the means of reviving religion among us. In wrath remember mercy."

This sets the stage for the drama of revival. Awakening can be anticipated when society degenerates to its lowest level, just when it seems there could never be a move of God. When disobedience, immorality, secularism, and godlessness prevails, the situation is ripe for revival. This sounds much like our current situation. Probably never have we been more in need.

Further, an awakening is essential when brotherly love wanes. The church also degenerates. We must ask, Where is the deep *koinonia* among the whole of God's people? There are small fellowship groups, but where is the spirit of *agape* love among *all* God's people? Finney states, "When there are dissensions, and jealousies, and evil speakings . . . then there is a great need of revival." [11] This, too, clearly speaks to our contemporary situation. I know of a church in my state that actually split some time ago over which side of the building to place the piano. It would be humorous if it weren't so sad.

When worldliness grips the church, a revival is desperately needed. In times past Christians have been sensitive about worldly plans and ways, ambitions, pleasures, and carnal values. Now it seems we have not only let down the barriers but we have become blasé about it also. We seem to be proud of our worldly attitudes and value systems and look with an air of superiority at the old morality and puritanical principles. I wonder how God really feels about that.

Open sin in the congregation demonstrates the need of new life, Finney tells us. Years ago church discipline— even if not well-handled at times—dealt with these issues. Now church members can commit adultery, deal deceitfully in business, curse and tell off-color stories. Honestly, what is done except to raise a few eyebrows? No wonder the world looks at the church with disdain, if not disgust.

Finally, when the lost are unconcerned, even when they hear the gospel, an awakening is sorely needed. In America at least, the gospel has all but saturated the nation. Radio, television, the printed page, all the media is deluged with gospel messages. Yet millions plunge on unheeding. Why? We need the presence of God in quickening power to make the gospel alive. Finney laid out these principles many years ago, yet their contemporary relevance is pungently obvious.

I know all this may sound somewhat negative. And I am sold on positive thinking and a sensible positive approach to spiritual realities. But I am also a realist. If we are in

need, we are in need—negative sounding or not. These realities *we must* face. Furthermore, the positive only becomes
positive because of the reality of true negatives. An awakening is a very positive thing, filled with positive blessings.
But I do not suppose we will experience the positive until
we come to grips with these negatives and are deeply burdened about them. Putting on superficially positive rose-col-
ored glasses will not make them go away.

If these are the conditions preceding a revival, as Finney
argues, when will the awakening come? That we have many
of these situations today is obvious. What do we lack? Finney
states revivals arrive when the "wickedness of the wicked
grieves and humbles and distresses Christians." [12] That Victorian expression simply means, when we finally get sick
and tired of the filth and moral corruption around us, God
will perhaps do something. What has caused us to make
peace with our sensual society? I suppose there are a thousand reasons; maybe it is simply because we are just so im-
mersed in it. But running the risk of sounding prudish—
and I dislike prudishness—we must be grieved over our social situation. Moral corruption has obliterated every civiliza-
tion in history, the classic case being Rome. Remember,
those who forget history are doomed to relive it. Homes
crumble, lives come apart, society disintegrates, and we go
down the drain. These statements are not old nineteenth-
century platitudes; the sociologists themselves speak in
alarm. Most serious of all, people stand under the judgment
of God. They desperately need forgiveness through Jesus
Christ. The powerful communication of the gospel is the
only hope. Revival must come!

Of course, it should be clear that it is *not* the reality
and presence of evil that precipitates awakenings. When
wickedness prevails, one of two things normally happens
to the church. Either the church grieves and begins to ago-
nize before God or the church makes peace with the situation and grows increasingly corrupt and compromising,

hence losing its testimony and power. Christians should *grieve* over the situation. If revival is to come, they must be deeply moved and distressed, Finney put it like this: "If Christians are made to feel that they have no hope but in God, and if they have sufficient feeling left to care for the honor of God, and the salvation of the souls of the impenitent, there will certainly be a revival." [13] Evil may abound, but if God's people prevail in prayer, the Lord will raise up a standard. Finney says, "I have known instances where a revival has broken in upon the ranks of the enemy, almost as suddenly as a clap of thunder, and scattered them—taking the very ringleaders as trophies, and breaking up their party in an instant." [14]

The Spirit of Prayer. This leads to another vital principle: An awakening comes when Christians have a deep, profound spirit of prayer for revival. I emphasized prayer earlier, but notice I say a spirit of prayer *for revival specifically.* Christians pray regularly and sincerely. But so often we ask for everything under the sun but revival. I have been in many evangelistic crusades and in countless prayer meetings for such efforts. I urge the participants to pray for revival. But people will pray for everything except that for which they are gathered. They pray for the sick, the missionaries, those in trouble, give thanks for the nice day, and on and on go the generalities. I become really discouraged at some prayer meetings. They are all but boring. Where is the spirit of prayer for an awakening? Where are the agonizers for a visitation of God? Where is the broken heart for the lost? Paul said, "My little children, with whom I am again in travail" (Gal. 4:19, RSV). Those who travail, prevail. That is the spirit that brings down heaven. I know I have belabored this point almost unmercifully; but when deep prayer concern grips hearts, there will surely be blessings.

The number of the burdened is often irrelevant to the degree of blessing. Finney tells of one dedicated woman in a church who became very burdened and anxious for the unconverted. She devoted herself to prayer for their salvation. Her distress and anxiety heightened until she pleaded with her pastor to call a special meeting to reach the lost. The minister put her off, he felt no such concern. She persisted—so did he. Finally she came to him and said, "If you do not appoint a meeting I shall die, for there is certainly going to be a revival." He relented and the next Sunday invited all who might be concerned for their salvation to a special meeting to seek God. He did not know of one concerned person. But to his amazement an unbelievable number responded. How did the dear woman know? The secret of the Lord was with her. Broken hearts and an agonizing prayer burden bring awakenings.

Where are we today? Does the spirit of prayer prevail? If not, then pray for the spirit of prayer. We probably need to begin by praying for power to pray. This spirit of prayer cannot be conjured up in the energy of the human. God's Spirit must come and lay this prayer burden on our souls.

Ministers Are the Key. Finney says that ministers must become burdened for revival. When this happens, the awakening may soon break. I served as a pastor for sixteen years. I have ministered to congregations all the way from small, rural congregations to large, urban churches. I know the demands on time, energy, and interest. A pastor and leaders are constantly pulled in a thousand different directions. How hard it is to keep focused on the essentials! Yet God has placed ministers in key leadership roles. Therefore, God's people tend to become what their leaders are. They adopt their leaders' views, system of values, styles of ministry, and sense of needs. A burdened pastor promotes a burdened congregation. A renewal-oriented leader develops a revival-oriented people.

Pastors have countless responsibilities. They all cry for attention; that I know. But pastors and leaders, I appeal to you as a fellow minister, get an awakening in your heart. You are the ones to develop this spirit in your people. Some will not understand. Some will think you should be giving attention to other concerns. But the Holy Spirit must be your guide. I know that thousands of demands will constantly press you, but set your face like a flint. And do not forget, when the awakening breaks, you will have a thousand committed laymen to meet those thousand demands. God probably never intended you to shoulder all those responsibilities anyway. God wants to bring life to the entirety of Christ's gifted body to meet the multiplicity of needs. I am sure, as I said, that an awakening is the only way the laity will come alive and meet those needs.

Lay people, you too must be deeply involved. Pray for your spiritual leaders. Love them. Understand them. Defend them. Hold up their hands. They need all the help and support you can give. Being a pastor can be a lonely life, even in the midst of countless people. Pray for them; pray for yourself. Pray God will give us all the burden for revival.

Sacrifice Is Central. Finney goes on to remark that awakening comes when Christians are found willing to make the necessary sacrifices to carry it on. We must face it: sacrifices are great. It will cost time and energy. It can cost reputation and material gain. People will be baffled as to what's going on; some will be very resistant. One must be willing to forfeit his "respect" among the world's crowd. God will not allow any limits to be imposed; we cannot tell God what we will and won't do. If we hold back our time, efforts, image, or anything, the Holy Spirit will be grieved and that will end the awakening.

I was preaching once in a small Texas town. The Spirit of God moved and probed deeply for three days. Then I attempted to lay the revival price of cleansing and fullness upon the church. There was strong resistance. It was quite remarkable. The Holy Spirit was so obviously grieved that the rest of the week was as spiritually cold as the proverbial iceberg. I felt we were merely going through the motions. I had never experienced anything quite like it before—or since, at least to that depth. There is a price to pay, and God's people must pay it if revival is to come.

God Does the Work

It is important to understand that we must permit God to promote the awakening in any way and by whatever instruments *he chooses*. At times we are very willing to have a revival provided we run it as we see fit. But God will not be hamstrung. He has his ways. They may be quite different from ours. He will often take the most unlikely people and thereby glorify himself. It was surely true in Corinth:

> For consider your call, brethren; not many of you were wise according to worldly standards, not many were powerful, not many were of noble birth; but God chose what is foolish in the world to shame the wise, God chose what is weak in the world to shame the strong, God chose what is low and despised in the world, even things that are not, to bring to nothing things that are, so that no human being might boast in the presence of God (2 Cor. 1:26–29, RSV).

The Holy Spirit laid his hands on a simple, uneducated shoe salesman and molded him into the great D. L. Moody; lifted up a drunken baseball player off a Chicago street and made him Billy Sunday, evangelist; touched a lanky North Carolina farm boy and fashioned a Billy Graham, who has preached the gospel to more people than anyone in the history of Christianity.

Means as well as men may be far different from our expectations. Often the Baptists think it *must* be a Baptist revival, and the Methodists a Methodist awakening, and the Pentecostals a Pentecostal one. I suppose we all feel our programs and means of ministry are the best, and God will surely choose them. Yet God will choose what and whom he pleases. God's way may well shock us all—especially the religious establishment. Still, we must let God control the awakening. His wisdom is best and his means will always bring the greatest amount of glory to himself. In a word, we must be honestly humble and let God be God.

God's Providence

Finally, we can expect a revival, as Finney expressed it, when God's providence indicates an awakening is about to dawn. At times the signs are explicit and plain; other times they are obscure. Yet there is something of a conspiring of events that the spiritually sensitive can discern. When the above principles are at work, openly or quietly, a revival is in the wings. I think we would all agree that much in today's world indicates God is longing to give us an awakening. If we can open our eyes to see, it becomes very clear: *God is at work*. That should give us all great encouragement.

Conclusion

Let me draw the curtain on the theme with a potent passage from Finney. It sums up all I have tried to say in this chapter and leads into the next.

Strictly I should say that when the foregoing things occur, a revival, to the same extent, already exists. In truth a revival should be expected whenever it is needed. If we need to be revived it is our duty to be revived. If it is duty it is possible, and we should set about being revived ourselves, and, relying on the promise of Christ to be with us in making disciples always and everywhere, we ought to labor to revive Christians and convert sinners, with confident expectation of success. Therefore, whenever the church needs reviving they ought and may expect to be revived, and to see sinners converted to Christ. When those things are seen which are named under the foregoing heads, let Christians and ministers be encouraged and know that a good work is already begun. *Follow it up.* [15]

7
It Can Happen Again; Putting It All Together

"Follow it up," Finney urged. How? we inquire. This final chapter will try to answer that fundamental question and "put it all together."

The Recipe for Revival

The "divine mix" that always seems to ferment revival is now clear: a desperate need, a willing God who is providentially maneuvering circumstances to a climax, and a dedicated handful of prevailing prayer warriors who will intercede until the revival dawns. In a word, a spiritual praying band and the sovereignty of God form the warp and woof of awakenings. That recipe always provides bread for the hungry.

Prayer Power

At the outset, I must say yet another word about the warp of our recipe, the centrality of prayer. I have become absolutely convinced that lack of prayer is the only reason revival has not yet come in our day. Unless we add that leaven in our spiritual lump, the recipe for revival is ruined and the bread for the hungry will never rise. Prayer is the channel through which awakenings always flow. This we have clearly seen over and again. Bernard of Clairvaux spent months in seclusion every year seeking God. Then he moved out on a six months preaching mission that rocked every city he entered. Martin Luther expended hours and hours in prayer. David Brainerd agonized on his knees in deep snow, coughing blood from tubercular lungs, soaking wet with perspiration, as he interceded for the American Indians. Missionary John "Praying" Hyde poured out his soul four hours a day begging God for revival in India where he labored. When an autopsy was performed after his untimely death, although a malignancy had taken him, it was discovered that his physical heart had actually shifted some distance in his chest cavity because of his agonizing hours of prayer.

In John Wesley's London home, I have stood in a tiny room with its single kneeling bench where Wesley spent the early hours every day interceding for the English awakening. I was so moved as I recalled the events of those great days of revival that I could not help falling on my knees on that old kneeling bench and asking God to do it again. What is it going to take for it to happen in our time I again ask? The answer is so simple: no prayer—no revival; much prayer—much blessings. As Samuel Chadwick expressed it:

There is no power like that of prevailing prayer—of Abraham pleading for Sodom, Jacob wrestling in the stillness of the night, Moses standing in the breach, Hannah intoxicated with sorrow, David heartbroken with remorse and grief, Jesus in sweat of blood. Add to this list from the records of the church your personal observation and experience, and always there is the cost of passion unto blood. Such prayer prevails. It turns ordinary mortals into men of power. It brings power. It brings fire. It brings rain. It brings life. It brings God.[1]

God Is Sovereign

If prayer is the warp of awakening, the woof is a sovereign God acting in the desperate human situation. We surely have the desperate situation today. Who can doubt that? And God is surely at work; any discerning believer can see that. His sovereign providence cries aloud, "This is the hour." That is why I say *all we need is prayer.* God is ready, but where, oh, where, is the dedicated band of interceders? Where is the remnant that always saves the situation? Where are those spiritual few who will pray until the dawn breaks? Are there any men and women of prayer who love God? Can they be found? Where are they?

The answer to this most basic essential question should be obvious. Has not the renewal, charismatic, deeper life, and other profound movings of the Holy Spirit given the contemporary church that very band of dedicated believers who could serve as God's praying remnant to precipitate a general great awakening? Surely this is true. What a potential the church has today in the renewed people of God, even if they be few in number. I hope we can see the importance and centrality of that statement. Actually, *this is the theme to which this entire book has been moving.* In renewed believers there exists the possibility of a great revival. Instead of being content with only a mere remnant of renewal and revival, leaving the mainstream of the church unmoved, why cannot that deepened, gifted, Spirit-filled remnant become the prayer channel for a great encompassing awakening? That seems so obvious that it just jumps out at one. In the light of this most important concept, I want to say a personal word to each one who has by any means whatever entered into a personal, renewed walk with God.

The Prayer for Revival

R. A. Torrey, a great man of intercession and instrument of revival, presents in his helpful volume *The Power of Prayer* the practicalities of prayer. Using as a pattern the experience of the early Jerusalem Church as they prayed for Peter's release from prison (Acts 12), he outlines prevailing prayer principles. If ever the church interceded successfully and saw God do a miracle work, it was when they prayed Peter out of prison. How did they pray? The Bible tells us, "Prayer was made without ceasing of the church unto God for him" (Acts 12:5).

"Unto God"

First of all, effective prayer is "unto God." That sounds rather ridiculous even to mention. We know that! But do we? Torrey said, "I do not believe that one in a hundred of the prayers of Protestant believers are really *unto God.*"[2] That may be an overstatement, but stop and think for a moment. Are we not often guilty of being far more concerned over what we are asking or how we are phrasing our requests than the great God we are addressing? Even more trite, do we not at times find ourselves just stringing a series of clichés together that sound good but say very little? I despair over some of the prayers I hear in our worship services. I do not want to appear unkind, but our public prayers are often little more than the "vain repetitions" our Lord warned us to avoid.

When we take the name of God on our lips, we must be vividly conscious to whom we speak. He is the mighty Creator; he is the powerful Sustainer; he is the gracious Redeemer; he is God Almighty, the sovereign Lord. Much of our contemporary sentimental songs and caricatures of God have clouded the nature of this sovereign Lord of might and power. He is not "the Man upstairs," nor "someone up there who likes you," as the church crooners whine out. He is the mighty God of consuming holiness.

Therefore, we must pause before we rush pell-mell unto God. We should linger long enough to question whether we are even worthy to stand in the presence of the One of whom the cherubim cry continually, "Holy, holy, holy is the Lord of hosts; the whole earth is full of his glory" (Isa. 6:3, RSV). Perhaps we should wait until we are ready to steal away, head bowed, heartbroken, saying, "I am not worthy, I have no right to be here. Woe is me."

Yet it is at this point of a contrite heart that the Lord Jesus can say to us, "Hitherto you have asked nothing *in my name;* ask, and you will receive, that your joy may be full" (John 16:24, RSV, author's italics). That is the key to worthy prayer; *in my name*. We make our requests in Jesus' name. What does it mean to pray in Christ's name? It must imply more than just a pious phrase tacked on the end of our prayers.

Prayer in Jesus' Name

Many make heavy sledding of the idea. Yet it is so simple. Torrey tells us, "It means simply this; that you ask the thing that you ask from the person of whom you ask it, on the ground of some claim that the person has in whose name you ask it." [3] For example, if we write a check for a person and have sufficient funds in our account to cover it, the person can cash it and receive the proceeds. But when we go to the bank of heaven, we have no account. We cannot cash a check in any amount on our own signature. However, Jesus Christ has infinite resources, and he has given us authority to write checks in his name on his account. We sign his name to the draft, and it is immediately paid from God's riches in glory.

Put it this way: we have no claims on God whatsoever. God owes us nothing and we deserve nothing. In ourselves we simply have no right to stand before him. But in Jesus' name, who has all "claims" on God, being the Son of God and Savior of the world, we can ask for anything in the light of his claims. "And when we draw near to God in that way we can get 'whatsoever' we ask; no matter how great it may be," as Torrey put it.[4] In other words, we stand in Christ's worthiness and righteousness.

Therefore, praying in Jesus' name certainly is no mere phrase we just add to prayer. It is an expression of a vitally important attitude and stance before God. We do not pray to the Father, "In thy name!": and we surely should never end our prayers with a simple "amen." We pray in Jesus Christ's name who enables us to stand before God. Because of his life, death, and resurrection, he is our worthiness. In the strong name of Jesus we can confidently make any claim whatsoever, so long as it is *in God's will.*

Praying in the Will of God

"In God's will"; that is another vital principle in coming "unto God." Someone has expressed it like this: "Christian prayer is God-centered, not self-centered. It's not getting things from God: it's finding out what God wants and getting ourselves into cooperation with that."

In praying unto God for an awakening, the issue immediately arises, Is it God's will to send a true revival? How can we know? We discover the will of God in various ways, not the least of which is to search the Scriptures and seek a word from the Lord. What does the Bible say about awakenings?

Lord, thou wast favorable to thy land;/thou didst restore the fortunes of Jacob./Thou didst forgive the iniquity of thy people;/ thou didst pardon all their sin./Thou didst withdraw all thy wrath; thou didst turn from thy hot anger./Restore us again, O God of our salvation,/and put away thy indignation toward us! Wilt thou be angry with us for ever?/Wilt thou prolong thy anger to all generations?/Wilt thou not revive us again,/that thy people may rejoice in thee?" (Ps. 85:1–6).

O Lord, I have heard the report of thee,/and thy work, O Lord, do I fear./In the midst of the years renew it;/in the midst of the years make it known;/in wrath remember mercy (Hab. 3:2).

The Lord is not slow about his promise as some count slowness, but is forbearing toward you, not wishing that any should perish, but that all should reach repentance (2 Pet. 3:9).

These passages along with a multitude of others cry to us that God longs to send a glorious awakening.

Providence also points to the purpose of God. Does the providence of God indicate a revival is *imminent?* Are there any harbingers of an awakening on the providential horizon? Throughout these pages, I have attempted to give an emphatic *yes* to this question. One more evidence to add to the many already presented: never in my entire ministry

have I received so many invitations to speak on the subject
of revivals or seen so much interest in awakenings. Everywhere people are coming alive to the need. *Time* magazine
in reporting on religious polls is even talking about a "Third
Great Awakening." Surely all of this interest is of God. No
longer are the advocates of a spiritual awakening a lone
voice crying in a wilderness of unconcern. These facts, plus
the multitude of others I have mentioned, would seem to
indicate this is God's sovereign hour.

Conclusion? We can pray in all confidence and assurance
for a profound revival because "this is the confidence which
we have in him, that if we ask anything according to his
will he hears us. And if we know that he hears us in whatever
we ask, we know that we have obtained the requests made
of him" (1 John 5:14–15, RSV). Praying in the known will
of God always leads to a confident prayer of faith.

The Prayer of Faith

Prayer unto God that prevails must always be believing
prayer. It honors God to ask in faith. Unbelief is a sin; it
casts doubt on the very veracity of God's Word. The Bible
is full of this faith principle. James said,

"Let him ask God who gives to all men generously. . . . But let
him ask in faith, with no doubting, for he who doubts is like a
wave of the sea that is driven and tossed by the wind. For that
person must not suppose that a double-minded man, unstable in
all his ways, will receive anything from the Lord" (Jas. 1:5–8, RSV).

But we must admit we do not always find it easy to
pray faith's prayer. Two things are normally necessary to
rise to that realm of confidence in prayer. One, we need
to know that what we ask for is God's desire. This point I
have already belabored: God does desire to pour out an
awakening. Secondly, we usually have to pray long enough
that the Holy Spirit can give us the inner assurance that
our prayer is heard. This point needs stressing in our day
of instant everything, including prayer. Perhaps we have

not prevailed in prayer because we have simply given up too soon. E. M. Bounds reminds us:

> We are ever ready to excuse our lack of earnest and toilsome praying. . . . We often end praying just where we ought to begin. We quit praying when God . . . is waiting for us to really pray. We are deterred by obstacles from praying as we submit to difficulties and call it submission to God's will.[5]

One of the greatest meetings I was ever in took place several years ago. In Birmingham, Alabama, a local church had invited me to preach in an evangelistic campaign. On Saturday, before the first service began Sunday morning, we fasted and prayed all day. How God blessed that effort. I shall never forget the glory of those seven days. My little church in Fort Worth, Texas, where I served as a young pastor, had an all-night chain of prayer every Saturday night. For a year we lived in a deep moving of the Spirit. There were times when God was so real that it was simply marvelous.

The great Welsh revival began by appointing a time of fasting and prayer in Cardiff and other towns in Wales. Torrey states it was in that setting the Holy Spirit fell mightily on Evan Roberts, God's key spokesman in the awakening. That sparked the blazing fires of revival that swept up the Rhondda Valley converting thousands. The secret of it all was they prayed *until the answer came*. The point is *they prevailed.*

Praying in the Spirit

Perhaps the whole beautiful picture of prevailing praying unto God can be summarized in Paul's phrase, "praying in the Spirit" (Eph. 6:18). The Holy Spirit is the teacher in God's school of prayer. He is the one who inspires, instructs, leads, enables, and directs the God-centered prayers of God's people to God's throne room. The Holy Spirit actually prays through the submissive believer and lifts both the prayer and person praying, right into God's glorious presence. He intercedes with "groanings which cannot be uttered" (Rom. 8:26). Therefore, all prevailing prayer begins and ends in the believer's openness and yieldedness to the moving of the Spirit to prayer. We must listen to his voice; he knows how to pray *unto God!*

"With Intense Earnestness"

The Revised Standard Version translates the second phrase in our key verse, "intense earnestness." The pungent word Luke used was *ektenos;* translated literally it means "stretched-out-edly." It pictures a person stretched out in an intensity of earnestness as he prays unto God. In a word, we are to pray from a burdened, broken, contrite, and agonizing heart.

Why do we find it so difficult to generate that kind of spirit and attitude in prayer? The Bible is clear concerning God's concern for the contrite heart: "The sacrifice acceptable to God is a broken spirit; a broken and contrite heart, O God, thou wilt not despise" (Ps. 51:17, RSV). The psalmist David saw it plainly. Note how he grasped the principle; it was in the context of brokenness over sin. Psalm 51 is a great hymn of confession. Could it be that sin sidetracks us from experiencing the broken praying heart that God so signally honors?

Such was surely the situation in the Hebrides awakening of 1949. I have already shared the story of the small group of men on the northern island of Lewis who were praying for revival in a barn outside their village. Remember, they had covenanted with God that they would "give Him no rest until He had made Jerusalem a praise in the earth." Months ticked away—nothing happened—but they continued to pray. On and on they interceded for a great awakening, still the heavens were silent. Then one night a young man arose from his knees and read Psalm 24:3–5. "Who shall ascend into the hill of the Lord? or who shall stand in his holy place? He that hath clean hands, and a pure

heart . . . He shall receive the blessing from the Lord."
The young man looked on his praying friends and said,
"Brethren, it is just so much humbug to be waiting night
after night, month after month, if we ourselves are not right
with God. I must ask myself, 'Is my heart pure? Are my
hands clean?' " At these words the Holy Spirit fell mightily
upon the group. Deep conviction and heartrending confession followed. Then came the outpouring of joy. The revival
had come. By this time it was in the early hours of the morning. They walked back to their community, rejoicing to discover almost the entire village awake, gathered at the police
station. They learned that the very moment the Holy Spirit
had fallen on them in the barn, he also fell on the unbelievers
in the village and woke them up in deep conviction. Everyone arose, dressed, and gathered at the police station asking
how to be saved. This raises the question, Why didn't they
go to the church? Regardless, it was only a matter of hours
until virtually the entire village was converted.

Never forget, "If I regard iniquity in my heart, *the Lord
will not hear me"* (Ps. 66:18, author's italics). The first step
to a broken, earnest prayer for revival is the prayer of confession. In the final analysis, our whole walk with God is dependent on dealing properly with our sins. Sin is a real problem,
even to believers. It is not an overstatement to say that
sin is the only obstacle to true revival praying.

A Real Problem

Most of us are willing to admit that we are far from
perfect. Yet we do not always see the seriousness of sin.
We tend to excuse ourselves, rationalize, blame others, or
retreat into the fact that we are saved and our sins in that
sense are forgiven. But sin is a problem—a real problem.
It can rupture our fellowship with God and others and hence
destroy our fervency in prayer—our entire spiritual life consequently suffers. Sin is a "fellowship problem" for believers.
The Scriptures make it clear:

If we say we have fellowship with him while we walk in darkness, we lie and do not live according to the truth; but if we walk in the light, as he is in the light we have fellowship with one another, and the blood of Jesus his Son cleanses us from all sin. If we say we have no sin, we deceive ourselves, and the truth is not in us. If we confess our sins he is faithful and just, and will forgive our sins and cleanse us from all unrighteousness (1 John 1:6–9, RSV).

John is obviously telling us one cannot walk in sin's darkness and God's light at the same time. Sin will inevitably extinguish the light of God's conscious presence and darken our whole spiritual experience.

The Real Issue

How are we to deal, therefore, with our personal sin that our Christian experience in general and our prayer life in particular might be all it should be? That is the issue! The first truth to grasp is found in 1 John 1:7, "If we walk in the light, as he is in the light, we have fellowship one with another, and the blood of Jesus his Son cleanses us from all sin." This simply means that if we would walk in the light, we must be constantly cleansed by the power of Christ's forgiveness. The death of Jesus is not applicable to the conversion experience alone. His sacrifice is to be effectual *every day*. Constant cleansing of our sins is what dispels our darkness, enabling us to walk in the fellowship of light.

I imagine this principle will find a reasonable acceptance by most Christians. Yet, it is right here that nebulous thinking often creeps in. Although the bulk of believers probably agree to the need of daily cleansing, too few have seemingly grasped the biblical patterns of how the believer is to deal with sin in order that the blood of Christ may cleanse and thus keep one in fellowship with God.

How to Deal with Personal Sin

At the outset it is most important to acquire a proper understanding of how sin invades life's basic interpersonal relationships. Sin always strikes at relationships and exerts itself in one of three ways. First of all, some sins involve the individual Christian alone and his fellowship with God. Secondly, there are sins that involve the Christian's fellowship with another individual. Although every sin is basically and essentially an affront to God, at times there are other individuals involved. Thirdly, there are occasions where one's sins are known and open and thus touch a group of people, such as the church.

Christians are not to view their daily sins as an ill-defined, nebulous, indefinite whole. This approach to sin tends to prevent one from dealing with the problem according to God's prescribed pattern. We must see our sins specifically, individually, and in the realm of their offense. This is most important because the Bible deals with sins on this basis. Therefore, as each individual sin is classified into one of the three interpersonal relational categories, it can be dealt with properly.

The Meaning of Confession

Take first the problem of sin that involves the believer alone and his personal fellowship with God. What does the Bible say about this situation? First John 1:9 states, "If we confess our sins, he is faithful and just, and will forgive our sins and cleanse us from all unrighteousness" (RSV). Confession brings cleansing. The word "confess," obviously the key term in this verse, is a most interesting word. In the original language, it is a compound word, that is, two different words put together to convey a new deep truth. It is composed of the verb "to say" with the prefix "the same." This implies that to confess sins is "to say the same as," or "to assent to," or "agree with." But with whom do we agree concerning our sins? The answer is obvious, the Holy Spirit. The Spirit of God is the one who puts his finger on our specific and individual sins. Therefore, when Christians confess sins, they "concede to" or "agree with" the voice of God's Spirit that some particular act truly is a sin. This precludes a generalized, indefinite acknowledgment of sins. For example, we often pray, "Lord, forgive me all my sins!" This is not the precise way the Bible says a Christian is to confess. To confess sins is to name them individually, one by one, agreeing with the Spirit of God that the particular act of which he convicts actually is a sin. We do not commit our sins as a big nebulous whole; they are individual acts of rebellion. Thus the confession of our sins should not be done in a general, ill-defined manner.

This normally means we must linger before God and stay in his presence until the Holy Spirit can search us out, convict us, and place his finger on those particular deeds that grieve him. But having acknowledged them before God in this prescribed manner, we have the assurance that the blood of Jesus cleanses them.

Making Out a "Sin Account"

Perhaps it will be helpful to share a personal experience here. An elderly, retired missionary lady spoke one time in our church. She brought a message on confession along the lines I have attempted to lay out. In the course of her address she urged us all to make out what she called a "sin account." We were to take a piece of paper and in the left-hand column write down several numbers. Then in the quiet of a secret place before God, we were to pray that the Holy Spirit would reveal every single thing that we had never honestly dealt with that was marring our fellowship with God. As a Christian I wanted to be led into all that God has for me, so I took her seriously. I made out my personal "sin account." To my humbling, the Spirit of God brought to my mind unconfessed sins that I had committed months, even years before. The Holy Spirit thoroughly searched me. I found much to deal with in my life. I wrote down everything. Then one by one I brought them back before God and acknowledged with the convicting Holy Spirit that those things were actually sins of which I was guilty. When I finally got honest, how precious the blood of Christ became!

This was not a time of morbid, neurotic introspection that some seem to enjoy. I must make this quite clear. We must never permit ourselves to indulge in that game. It was simply an honest evaluation of myself before a holy God. Therefore, it brought great release. It was actually one of the most liberating experiences of my Christian walk. I experienced a new fellowship with God. I felt something like Isaiah must have felt after his humbling experience of God when the Lord's word came to him: "your guilt is taken away, and your sin forgiven" (Isa. 6:7, RSV).

Sin Against Others

God's forgiveness is glorious. But we have also seen that some sins strike at our relations to others as well as to God. In such instances, to confess to God alone is insufficient to experience the full liberty of Christ's forgiveness. We should confess them to God, of course, but Jesus stated that if you sin against another and "are offering your gift at the altar, and there remember that your brother has something against you, leave your gift there before the altar and go; first be reconciled to your brother, then come and offer your gift" (Matt. 5:23-24, RSV).

I do not think we can avoid the simple truth presented here. If we refuse to acknowledge sins against individuals and fail to seek restoration of fellowship, we cannot really expect deep fellowship with God—or with one another.

This truth came home to me several years ago. A young, deeply spiritual man preached on this theme in the church where I was pastor. The Spirit of God bore profound witness to us all. Many were compelled by the Holy Spirit to put things right. I, too, found I had sinned against some individuals and to be honest with God and myself I knew I must right the wrong. I admit, it was really difficult. Pride dies hard. But I knew if I were to have real peace in my heart, I must do it. I soon found myself seeking out one of my

Christian brothers. I suppose my sin against him was not of the worst nature. I just had lost love and fellowship with him. So I went to him to acknowledge my error and seek his forgiveness. God really searched me out and helped me get many things right. I even had to send some money in a letter to put one situation straight. But after all, that was the only honest, ethical thing to do. God seeks our honesty and willingness to follow his leading with true humility and brokenness over that which destroys our fellowship with him and others. It is not fanaticism, it is honesty and integrity.

Let it again be made clear that I do not speak of a morbid introspective seeking and digging out of past sins. It is just being objective with oneself. Furthermore, it is necessary because the Spirit of God is grieved over unconfessed sin and ruptured human relationships. God is light; we must take our darkness seriously. Seeking forgiveness from those against whom we have sinned is clearly essential to walking in fellowship with one another; "that which we have seen and heard we proclaim also to you, so that you may have fellowship with us" (1 John 1:3, RSV). If God expects us to confess our sins to him to have fellowship with himself, certainly the principle applies to our human, interpersonal relationships. If there could be something of a real openness among ourselves, if we could affirm one another, and embrace one another in the arms of confession in the context of a true binding of our lives in love, understanding, and forgiveness, our homes, our churches, and our nation would be revolutionized. That is surely what *koinonia,* fellowship, in the biblical sense means—and that is not far from a spiritual awakening.

Sin and the Church

Finally, we find that at times sin is open, obvious, and others know of it. Or we may have some particular distressing problem, secret or otherwise, where we have constant difficulties. How are these issues to be dealt with? James told us, "Confess your sins to one another, and pray for one another, that you may be healed" (5:16, RSV). Does James mean to imply that there are times when we should confess some of our sins to someone or perhaps even to a group in the church? This seems to be his meaning. There should be that person or group in the fellowship of believers to whom we can be quite open, honest, and candid about ourselves. This is really what the "fellowship of kindred minds" means. Our churches should always be a fellowship of love and understanding where we feel unthreatened to open up our real selves to our brothers in Christ.

I have witnessed marvelous times of fellowship and healing on that basis. I have been in groups where genuine communion in the Spirit prevailed. One could truly be a real person and share in all honesty. We need this kind of fellowship in Christ. I have seen God's Spirit probe deeply among his people. Confession actually broke out. But what a time of healing and fellowship it was for the church. Many of the Christians were never the same again. Surely this is the kind of honesty that God honors and uses to revive his work. All great revivals have begun something like that.

A Word of Caution

We must be most careful here however. This exercise can easily degenerate into confessing for confession's sake. Some have fallen into this trap. That can become very negative and damaging to health and fellowship. I should suppose that there are some areas of our lives that only God should ever know. Of course, if one's sins are so gross and well-known that reproach is brought upon the entire church and thus the fellowship of the church is broken, then forgiveness should obviously be sought from the entire church. This is what lies behind the principle of church discipline that many congregations have apparently forgotten today. Perhaps the best rule of thumb is that the confession should be made in the realm of the offense, and the Holy Spirit will guide otherwise.

Now when we get honest before God and others as directed by the Word and the Spirit, we can claim God's promise: "He is faithful and just, and will forgive our sins and cleanse us from all unrighteousness" (1 John 1:9, RSV). Being forgiven implies a debt remitted, cleansing speaks of a stain bleached out. God not only forgives us, he cleanses us from even the stain of the memory and thus sets us free to walk in the light as he is in the light.

When we permit God to exercise our hearts on these issues, we will begin to get to the core of that contrite, broken, intense prayer the Jerusalem church offered to God. And that kind of praying paves the way for real revival.

"Of the Church"

The third primary principle of great revival praying points up the fact that the church—not just an individual—is God's method in revival praying. God of course answers individual prayers. But there is great prayer power in the united people of God interceding for needs. Jesus said, "If *two of you* shall agree on earth as touching any thing that they shall ask, it shall be done" (Matt. 18:19-20, KJV, author's italics). It is unified praying that God longs to hear.

But we retort, We will never get the whole church on its knees. Probably true! Yet Jesus only asked for two. Surely there are at least two genuinely renewed people who can pray. You who read these words are probably one. Have you been deepened through the renewal, charismatic, deeper life, or some other movement or experience? You are not alone. There is at least one other you can find who will join you in prayer for awakening. No doubt there are many if we will seek them out.

But the rest of the church will not understand, you say. That is also likely true. But then they never have. The *ecclesia* in the *ecclesia,* the faithful remnant, has always been

God's way of precipitating powerful movements. If we wait for everyone to be deepened and ready for blessings, we may wait forever. And if that ever did happen, we would not need an awakening; it would have already occurred. Furthermore, when the dawn breaks on revival, those who criticize now will understand, join in, and rise up to call you blessed.

My plea to you, therefore, is to find that renewed handful and set yourselves to prayer. You probably already know who they are. If not, God's Spirit will surely lead you to those of like burden. It may well be that is why God has renewed you in the first place. Be the catalyst in the group. If *you* do not engage in prevailing prayer, who will? No man is greater than his prayer life. If your renewal is truly of the Holy Spirit, it will thrust you into intercession. The kind of revival we need may well wait for you.

> There's a high and holy vocation
> Needing workers everywhere
> 'Tis the highest form of service
> It's the ministry of prayer.

"For Him"

The final key phrase in our revival prayer verse is, "for him." The church earnestly prayed for Peter and his release. That is, the request was definite, pointed, singular, *answerable*. Will I sound unspiritual if I say God himself can hardly answer some of our prayers? They are often vague, deal only in generalities, and really say nothing definite. If an answer did come, we would probably not recognize it. Vague prayers sound good; stringing together clichés in the language of Zion may make a favorable impression on the uninitiated, but God urges us to ask for something specific and real, that which meets genuine needs. If you cannot write down your request and check it off when the answer comes, it probably isn't the right kind of prayer.

Here are some definite scriptural prayers for revival:

Lord, convict me of my specific sins that need cleansed in the blood (see 1 John 1:9).

Lord, give me the Spirit of prevailing prayer (see Rom. 8:26).

Lord, burden me deeply over the headlong rush to destruction many engage in (see Rom. 9:1–3).

Lord, pour out your Holy Spirit mightily upon us (see Acts 4:31).

Lord, revive your work in the midst of years (see Hab. 3:2).

That's the kind of intercessions that God's great compassionate heart desires to hear.

Why all this insistence on prayer? Why all this urging to be the initiator of a prevailing prayer group? Andrew Bonar had it right: "O brother, pray; in spite of Satan, pray; spend hours in prayer; rather neglect friends than not pray; rather fast, and lose breakfast, dinner, tea and supper—and sleep too—than not pray. And we must not talk about prayer, we must pray in right earnest. The Lord is near. He comes softly while the virgins slumber." [6] God *needs* a faithful, praying band of prevailing believers.

A Word to Ministers of the Gospel

What I have tried to say to this point clearly applies to all God's people, for all God's people are responsible to do his will. But there is a special word to pastors, preachers, ministers: those in the places of leadership. Preachers and leaders, you are especially responsible for revival. God has placed you in a unique place in his church. You are to epitomize all an awakening stands for.

Preaching

Powerful proclamation has always been a vital central element in great awakenings. The health curve of the church can be traced by the health curve of great biblical preaching. Preachers are to *preach*. Although preaching has been in the doldrums for several decades, it is once more coming

to the forefront. Even in our age of mass media and techno-
logical communication, nothing yet devised can make an
impact like a Spirit-filled man of God bringing a solid, scriptural sermon from a burning heart. There will never be a
substitute for that. This is because preaching is actually an
event. Pulpit proclamation is not merely a means for convey-
ing the content of the Christian faith; it is an event wherein
God meets man. It is a form of God addressing himself to
persons. As H. H. Farmer has put it:

Preaching is telling me something. But it is not merely telling
me something. It is God actively probing me, challenging my will,
calling me for decision, offering one His succour, through the only
medium which the nature of His purpose permits Him to use,
the medium of a personal relationship. It is as though, to adopt
the Apostle's words, 'God did beseech me by you.' It is God's 'I—
thou' relationship with me carried on your 'I—thou' relationship
with me, both together coming out of the heart of His saving purpose which is moving on through history to its consummation in
His kingdom.[7]

Preaching in an Existential Situation

It is here that the distinctive nature of effective preaching appears. Preaching is almost a sacrament. Christian
preaching is unique because when it is true to its genius;
it is both uttered and listened to in faith. In the final analysis,
preaching is actually God's activity. It is God encountering
persons in the extreme and supreme crises of their lives.
Real preaching utterly depends upon the preacher convey-
ing the sense of the living, saving activity of God in Christ.

These principles of Christian preaching project a number of ideas. Initially, preaching must always be viewed as
a personal encounter. God himself confronts people in the
proclaimer on a Person-to-person level. As Farmer expresses
it, "God's 'I—thou' relationship with me is never apart from,
is always in a measure carried by, my 'I—thou' relationship
with my fellows."

This concept throws light on the position held by the

preacher in proclamation. First, he must be intimately related to God in an "I—thou" sense. If he loses the reality of God's presence in his preaching, all is lost. Secondly, he must also be related to his hearers in this "I—thou" manner of understanding relationships. The preacher stands, as it were, at the corner of a right-angled triangle. He is related vertically to God and horizontally to his hearers in the preaching situation. In the context of this setting God completes the triangle and confronts and addresses persons. Moreover, there is give and take on the part of the preacher in all directions on the triangle. It is an existential encounter par excellence. This is Christian preaching. This is *event*.

The immediate implication of this concept is that preaching is costly. Effective proclamation does not come easy. The preacher is totally giving himself on the horizontal plane to the people and vertically he pours out his very soul to God. He so gives of himself in the preaching experience that he is drained. Real preaching can be painful. The pulpit is not a place to be cool and casual in spirit and attitude. Paul said, "Therefore be alert, remembering that for three years I did not cease night or day to admonish every one with tears" (Acts 20:31, RSV).

Therefore, the preacher must keep God and his people in his preaching vision. As important as is the content of one's message, people are central. We do not preach in a vacuum. It is true, as James Stewart has said, "The Evangelist must be sure of his message." Perhaps in this age of uncertainty and relativity this is more important than ever, but preaching is to people. To real, hurting, hungry people we address our message in love, compassion, and understanding as we attempt to relate to them meaningfully.

Thus we conclude that preaching as I have described it is dynamically effective. The preacher must attempt to cultivate real preaching power because it is one of the prime settings in which God works. This approach to preaching can obviously make a real mark in spawning spiritual awakening.

Sermon Content

I have stressed the existential experience in preaching. I surely do not mean to downplay the content of our message however. Sermonic content is vital to effective revival preaching, to any great preaching for that matter. A preacher should say something. What is that *something?* In the first serious history of the Great Awakening published in 1842, Joseph Tracey tells us:

We cannot but also observe that the principal means of the late revival were, the more than ordinary preaching up such Scripture and most important doctrines as these, namely: The all seeing eye, purity, justice, truth, power, majesty and sovereignty of God; the spirituality, holiness, extent and strictness of his law; our original sin, guilt, depravity and corruption by the fall; including a miserable ignorance of God and enmity against him, our predominant and constant bent to sin and creatures above him; our impotence and aversion to return to him; our innumerable and heinous actual offenses, and thereby our horrid, aggravated guilt, pollution and odiousness in his eyes; his dreadful and efficacious wrath and curse upon us; the necessity that his law should be fulfilled, his justice satisfied, the honor of his holiness, authority and truth maintained in his conduct toward us; our utter impotence to help ourselves, and our continual hazard of being sent into endless misery; the astonishing displays of the absolute wisdom and grace of God in contriving and providing for our redemption; satisfaction, purchase and grace of Christ; the nature and necessity of regeneration to the holy image of God by the supernatural operation of the divine Spirit; with the various parts of his office in enlightening our minds, awakening our consciences, wounding, breaking, humbling, subduing and changing our hearts, infusing his saving graces, witnessing with our spirits that we are the children of God, and raising his consolations and joys in us; the difference between his saving graces and merely moral virtues without sanctification, whereby multitudes are deceived to their eternal ruin; in special, the nature and necessity of receiving Christ, so as to be actually united to him and have entire and everlasting interest in him, to be forthwith justified by his imputed righteousness, adopted into the number of the children of God, entitled to all their privileges assured in the covenant of grace, have Christ as our mediatorial and vital Head of all good, with his constant dwelling and acting by his Spirit in us; and then, in continual acts of faith, deriving from him fresh supplies of spiritual liveliness and comfort, as also light and strength for every duty and to carry on our sanctification; the nature of gospel obedience and holiness, and their necessity, not as the matter of our justification, but as the fruit and evidence of justifying faith, and to glorify God and enjoy him the principal end both of our creation and redemption; and lastly, the sovereignty of the grace of God in this whole transaction, from its original in the decree of election, to its consummation in glory.[8]

I know all that may sound ancient and puritanical to our modern ears, but that's the kind of content powerful preaching employs. It is not outmoded, Victorian, or irrelevant. The great truths that emerge from plunging deep into the Word of God are always alive. It is what people need. It is what they want. When we update these realities into contemporary language and relevant thought-forms, people will respond. Preachers are to preach the Word in power.

Holy Living

Do I need to say anything about a godly life? Robert Murray McCheyne was right: "A holy minister is an awful weapon in the hands of God." When one's service and ministry are finally summed up, that which makes the most lasting and vital impression is a Christlike life. As a young minister, I once had the opportunity of serving as an associate pastor to a true "man of God." He was not the pastor of a large, influential church. He was not an outstanding or eloquent preacher. His intellectual achievements were not extraordinary. Yet his ministry impacted over a large area. Many came to faith in Christ through his witness. The one fact of his ministry that was so outstanding and that which gave him such influence for Christ was the simple godliness of his life. He really was a holy man. And though he passed on some years ago, his influence still remains.

Two important issues are implied in the principle of a holy life. In the first place, the image of the servant of Christ is extremely relevant to the effectiveness of his ministry.

As Gavin Reid has pointed out, "Image communication can have an important role to play." Of course, this is true for any Christian, leader or layman. Paul said, "Brethren, join in imitating me, and mark those who so live as you have an example in us" (Phil. 3:17, RSV). When a man can honestly and humbly say that about himself, his life will prove powerful in ministry.

Secondly, one's native ability is not necessarily the determining factor in an effective ministry. Of course, God uses our talents as long as our life is totally committed to Christ. But a godly life always speaks. And even if we are "ten-talented," if our ministry does not reflect the holiness of Jesus Christ, God can use us but little.

It thus seems vitally important to me for all who aspire to be instrumental in revival to learn the principles of godly living. There will be those who do not understand. The worldly crowd—even the worldly crowd in the church—will criticize, perhaps scorn. *But they will never forget a real man or woman of God.* And when the crunch comes in their lives, as it inevitably will, the godly minister is the one they seek. People want their spiritual leaders to be holy men of God.

Leading

Leaders lead! But into what and where do they direct Christ's church? Leadership goals are multiplied. But in all your leading, ministers, direct people to God and spiritual realities. It is so perilously easy to strive toward every good thing except the one best thing: a deep experience of the living God. In the end if your people do not enjoy a profound walk with Jesus Christ, what do they have? At best it is a mere sanctified humanism, spiced up with fleshly fervor or shallow emotionalism, full of sound and fury *but with no reality,* signifying nothing. God save his ministers from leading his people up that primrose path.

Above all, ministers should lead their people in prayer.

Be an example yourself. It was said of Edwin Paycon, "prayer was preeminently the business of his life." Ravenhill reminds us: "The pastor who is not praying is playing; the people who are not praying are straying. The pulpit can be a shop-window to display one's talents; the prayer closet allows no showing off." [9] It was Zepp who cried, "God help us seek popularity where it counts—at the court of God." E. M. Bounds tells us: "It was claimed for Augustus Caesar that he found Rome a city of wood, and left it a city of marble. The pastor who succeeds in changing his people from a prayerless to a prayerful people, has done a greater work than did Augustus in changing a city from wood to marble. And after all, this is the prime work of the preacher. The preacher is not sent to merely induce men to join the church, nor merely to get them to do better. It is to get them to pray, to trust God, and to keep God ever before their eyes, that they may not sin against Him." [10]

Oh, preacher, lead your people to pray. Be the nucleus yourself of a praying band. Let the worldly in your church raise an eyebrow. Let your undiscerning fellow ministers turn away. The flock of God has been committed to your trust. You do not have to answer to the calloused, the worldly, or your peers. You must answer to God for your stewardship of the sheep. In all your leading, lead them to pray for revival.

A Final Word

This book has obviously been an appeal to prayer to all God's concerned people, ministers and laity alike. I have tried to stress the staggering need of a significant spiritual awakening that would hopefully sweep the whole church, nation, and world. It is not too much to hope, for God can do "exceeding abundantly above all that we ask or think" (Eph. 3:20). I have further attempted to make it vividly clear that this kind of mighty movement, from the human perspective, is brought about by prayer alone; and that usually by only a handful of the faithful. You who read these pages, whoever you are, you to whom God has spoken and through some means renewed and revived your spiritual experience; you are the key. May God gently slip you as his key into the prayer slot of his heavenly vault that will unlock the riches of his treasure store and thus enable the Holy Spirit to pour out his wealth on a very needy human situation. Christian, pray. Gather a prayer group around you. Intercede until the heavens open. The world languishes for an awakening. God waits for you at his throne. Claim the promise: "If my people who are called by my name humble themselves, and pray and seek my face, and turn from their wicked ways, then I will hear from heaven, and will forgive their sin and heal their land" (2 Chron. 7:14, RSV). That's the sort of revival we need. That's the kind of awakening that must come.

Notes

Chapter 1

1. Jonathan Edwards, *Sinners in the Hands of an Angry God* (Little Rock: The Challenge Press).

2. Mendell Taylor, *Exploring Evangelism* (Kansas City: Beacon Hill Press, 1964), p. 409.

3. Ibid., p. 410.

4. Ibid.

5. Ibid., p. 412.

Chapter 2

1. Elton Trueblood, *The Yoke of Christ* (New York: Harper and Row, 1958), p. 179.

2. G. Kittel, and G. Friedrich, eds., *Theological Dictionary of the New Testament*, Vol. III (Grand Rapids: William B. Eerdmans Publishing Company, 1965), p. 807.

3. Elton Trueblood, *Alternative to Futility* (New York: Harper and Row, 1948), p. 31.

4. The book title by Ray Stedman that outlines his entire program.

5. Trueblood, *The Yoke of Christ*, p. 39.

6. Ibid., p. 38.

7. Robert H. Schuller, pastor of Garden Grove Community Church, Anaheim, California.

8. Charles G. Finney, *Memoirs* (New York: Fleming H. Revell Company, 1876), pp. 163, 170, 171.

Chapter 3

1. Frank Stagg, E. Glenn Hinson, and Wayne E. Oates, *Glossolalia* (Nashville: Abingdon Press, 1967).

2. Ibid., p. 47.

3. Ibid., p. 53.

4. John Wesley, *A Plain Account of Christian Perfection* (London: The Epworth Press, 1952), p. 29.

Chapter 4

1. Mrs. W. E. Boardman, *Life and Labores of Reverend W. E. Boardman* (New York, 1887), p. vii.

2. W. B. Sloane, *These Sixty Years* (London: Pickering and Ingles, n. d.), p. 17.

3. Steven Barabas, *So Great Salvation* (Westwood, New Jersey: Fleming H. Revell Company, n. d.), p. 27.

4. *The Keswick Convention in Print*, p. 15.

5. Evan H. Hopkins, *The Law of Liberty in the Spiritual Life* (London: Marshall Brothers, 1905), p. 3.

6. Ibid., p. 4.

7. Barabas, op. cit., pp. 42–47.

8. Evan Hopkins, *The Law of Liberty in the Spiritual Life*, p. 8.

9. Ibid.

10. *The Keswick Week*, 1910, p. 82.

11. Gregory Mantle, *The Counterfeit Christ* (New York: Fleming H. Revell Company, 1920), p. 37.

12. Barabas, op. cit., pp. 65–66.

13. Ibid., p. 95.

14. *The Keswick Week*, 1902, p. 56.

15. *The Keswick Convention in Print*, 1941, p. 57.

16. Andrew Murray, *The Full Blessing of Pentecost* (New York: Fleming H. Revell Company, 1908), p. 110.

17. G. Campbell Morgan, *The Spirit of God* (New York: Fleming H. Revell Company, 1900), p. 194.

18. W. Graham Scroggie, *The Fulness of the Holy Spirit* (Chicago: Bible Institute Colportage Association, 1925), pp. 19–21.

Chapter 5

1. Gibson Winter, *The New Creation as Metropolis* (New York: The Macmillan Company, 1963), p. 25.

2. Ernest F. Stoeffler, *The Rise of Evangelical Pietism* (Leiden, Netherlands: E. J. Brill, 1971), p. 29.

3. Donald Bloesch, *The Evangelical Renaissance* (Grand Rapids, Michigan: William B. Eerdmans Publishing Company, 1973), p. 104.

4. Ernest F. Stoeffler, *Continential Pietism and Early American Christianity* (Grand Rapids, Michigan: William B. Eerdmans Publishing Company, 1976), p. 9.

5. Stoeffler, *The Rise of Evangelical Pietism*, p. 115.

6. Ibid., p. 9.

7. Bloesch, p. 106.

8. Ibid.

9. Ibid.

10. Ibid., p. 108.

11. Ibid.

12. Ibid., p. 109.

13. Stoeffler, *The Rise of Evangelical Pietism*, p. 131.

14. Bloesch, p. 110.

15. Ibid., p. 20.

16. Ibid., p. 116.

17. Ibid., p. 132.

18. Ibid., p. 122.

19. Ibid., p. 124.

20. Stoeffler, *The Rise of Evangelical Pietism*, p. 36.

21. Ibid., p. 51.

22. Ibid., p. 68.

23. Paulus Scharpff, *The History of Evangelism* (Grand Rapids, Michigan: William B. Eerdmans Publishing Company, 1966), p. 34.

24. Stoeffler, *The Rise of Evangelical Pietism*, p. 228.

25. Ibid.

26. B. K. Kuipes, *Church in History* (Grand Rapids, Michigan: William B. Eerdmans Publishing Company, 1948), p. 345.

27. Scharpff, *The History of Evangelism*, p. 42.

28. Ibid., pp. 44–45.

29. Stoeffler, *Continental Pietism and Early American Christianity*, p. 34.

30. Donald G. Bloesch, *The Crisis in Piety* (Grand Rapids: William B. Eerdmans Publishing Co., 1976), p. 38.

31. Donald G. Bloesch, *The Evangelical Renaissance*, p. 142.

32. Stoeffler, *The Rise of Evangelical Pietism*, p. 107.

33. Stoeffler, *Continental Pietism and Early American Christianity*, p. 56.

34. Ibid., p. 57.

Chapter 6

1. Robert E. Coleman, *One Divine Moment* (Old Tappan, New Jersey: Fleming H. Revell Company, 1970), p. 27.

2. James Burns, *Revivals: Their Laws and Leaders* (Grand Rapids, Michigan: Baker Book House, 1960), p. 24.

3. Coleman, op. cit., p. 69.

4. Ibid., p. 64.

5. Burns, op. cit., p. 28.

6. Robert E. Coleman, *Dry Bones Can Live Again* (Old Tappan, New Jersey: Fleming H. Revell Company, 1969), p. 35.

7. Burns, p. 38.

8. Ibid., p. 58.

9. Ellis A. Fuller, "The Primacy of Evangelism," *The Review and Expositor,* Vol. XLII, No. 1 (Louisville: Southern Baptist Theological Seminary, 1945), p. 3.

10. Burns, p. 44.

11. Charles G. Finney, *Revival Lectures* (New York: Fleming H. Revell Company, 1868), p. 23.

12. Ibid., p. 26.

13. Ibid., p. 27.

14. Ibid.

15. Ibid., p. 23.

Chapter 7

1. Samuel Chadwick as quoted by Leonard Ravenhill, *Revival Praying* (Minneapolis: Bethany Fellowship, Inc., 1962), p. 44.

2. R. A. Torrey, *The Power of Prayer* (Grand Rapids, Michigan: Zondervan Publishing House, 1955), p. 74.

3. Ibid., p. 135.

4. Ibid., p. 137.

5. Leonard Ravenhill, *A Treasury of Prayer* (Minneapolis: Bethany Fellowship, Inc., 1961), p. 52.

6. Leonard Ravenhill, *Why Revival Tarries* (Minneapolis: Bethany Fellowship, Inc., 1959), p. 130.

7. Herbert H. Farmer, *The Servant of the Word* (London: Nesbit, 1941), pp. 27–28.

8. Joseph Tracy, *A History of the Revival of Religion* (Boston: Tappan and Dennet, 1842), pp. 400–401.

9. Ravenhill, *Why Revival Tarries*, p. 7.

10. Ravenhill, *A Treasury of Prayer*, p. 128.